COOPERATE -

Advancing your nonprofit organization's mission through college & community partnerships

A GUIDE FOR NONPROFIT LEADERS

DR. NATHAN A. SCHAUMLEFFEL, EDITOR

ISBN: 0692296190
ISBN 13: 9780692296196
Library of Congress Control Number: 2014916923
Indiana Campus Compact, Indianapolis, Indiana

Indiana | Campus Compact

ABOUT INDIANA CAMPUS COMPACT

http://www.indianacampuscompact.org/

Mission

Indiana Campus Compact supports higher education's efforts to develop students into well-informed, engaged citizens. By providing programs, services, and resources, ICC serves as a catalyst for campuses and communities to improve people's lives through service-learning and civic engagement initiatives.

Membership

Indiana Campus Compact's (ICC's) membership includes public and private two- and four-year institutions committed to fulfilling the civic purposes of higher education. It is the only statewide higher education association dedicated solely to campus-based civic engagement. ICC promotes public and community service that develops students' citizenship skills; helps campuses forge effective, reciprocal community partnerships; and provides resources and training for faculty seeking to integrate civic and community-based learning into the curriculum.

Faculty Fellows Program

The Indiana Campus Compact Faculty Fellows program is a year-long learning community experience. Selected individuals serve a one-year term as part of a cohort with other engaged scholars from ICC member campuses. The program serves as a faculty professional-development model to support the integration of service-learning and community engagement into the three components of faculty development: teaching, research, and service. Funding for the Faculty Fellows program is provided by the Lilly Endowment Inc.

The overall goals of the program include

- supporting faculty in the practice of the scholarship of engagement;

- providing faculty with opportunities to collaborate with a community organization in a way that advances teaching and scholarship while addressing a significant social, economic, or environmental issue; and

- building a strong and productive social and intellectual community as a cadre of scholars.

Faculty Fellows

- teach a service-learning course within the program period;

- provide direct service to a nonprofit organization during the program year to assist in addressing a particular community issue that is related to his or her academic discipline or expertise as an educator; and

- work as a cadre to develop a research or creative project to enhance and advance the field of service engagement.

This book is a result of the academic year 2012–2013 Faculty Fellows class.

Suggested Citations

Chicago Style Suggested Citation
Schaumleffel, N. A., ed. *Cooperate—Advancing Your Nonprofit Organization's Mission Through College and Community Partnerships: A Guide for Nonprofit Leaders.* (Indianapolis: Indiana Campus Compact, 2014).

American Psychological Association (APA) Suggested Citation
Schaumleffel, N. A. (Ed.) (2014). *Cooperate - Advancing your nonprofit organization's mission through college & community partnerships: A guide for nonprofit leaders.* Indianapolis, IN: Indiana Campus Compact.

CONTENTS

FOREWORD

It is a pleasure to be able to introduce this work by Dr. Nathan A. Schaumleffel and his Indiana Campus Compact colleagues.

In an ever-changing world, especially for nonprofits, we are constantly looking for new ways to fully execute our mission. We spend so much time focused on what we've done; but we don't always devote as much energy to finding new ways to help accomplish our objectives. In this book, Nathan and his colleagues show us one way to connect with an energy source. This energy source is a group of talented people who are endeavoring to dedicate their careers to serving others.

Mario Morino, in his book *Leap of Reason*, advocates bluntly for nonprofits to do the hard work needed to improve their impact and to recruit culture leaders that can implement accountability. Mario exhorts all nonprofit leaders to find ways to innovate and more appropriately measure success.

To help with this innovation, many colleges have begun to offer programs in nonprofit education. A lesser number are focused on competency models that include hands-on learning. This book focuses on programs that encourage hands-on learning with authentic assessment and what Dr. Schaumleffel calls "nonprofit leadership they way it oughta be."

Nathan and his colleagues takes us through a methodical, step-by-step approach to attracting new talent to the nonprofit sector and supporting those already leading and managing nonprofit organizations. By helping people who want to serve in our sector, you can also help accomplish your organization's mission. The people you work with through these college and community partnerships are not retired file clerks. These students and campus volunteers are impassioned people who are working to improve the professionalism of our sector. The Indiana Campus Compact Faculty Fellows that authored this book gives a framework for interacting with local campuses to help ensure a steady pipeline of talented people who can help expand our reach.

We know this works. In our own organization we have successfully modeled programs for our constituents that are driven largely by paid interns. It is a win-win. The students gain valuable experience, professors get excellent professional development experiences, and we are able to stretch our precious budget dollars that much more. This allows us to do well for our organization and to do well by the students and the professors that serve their students and our organizations. Rarely do we get the opportunity to help others and to help ourselves at precisely the same time.

As we all seek to innovate and deliver more with fewer dollars, we urge you to consider the approach advocated in this fine work. To learn more about the Nonprofit Leadership Alliance and its Alliance Campus Partners, please visit http://www.nonprofitleadershipalliance.org

Michael Cruz, CNP
President Emeritus, Nonprofit Leadership Alliance
President, Lighthouse Advisors LLC

Susan Schmidt, MPA, CNP
President, Nonprofit Leadership Alliance

ABOUT THE AUTHORS

Dr. Nathan A. Schaumleffel, CNP, Associate Professor, Indiana State University

Dr. Schaumleffel is an Associate Professor of Recreation and Nonprofit Leadership and serves as Campus/Executive Director of the Nonprofit Leadership Alliance Certification Program at Indiana State University (ISU). He recently led the Indiana State University Nonprofit Leadership program to the 2013 Nonprofit Leadership Alliance–Sprint Campus Partner of the Year Award. He has been awarded both the Indiana State University Distinguished Faculty Award for Community-Based Learning and Scholarship and the Distinguished Faculty Service Award. Dr. Schaumleffel has served as an ICC Faculty Fellow in AY08-09 and AY11-12, and served as Senior Faculty Fellow for AY12–13 and AY13–14. He has also served as a Faculty Fellow for the Indiana State Center for Public Service and Community Engagement and the ISU Foundation. In practice, some of the community organizations in which he engages students are Autism Speaks, Boy Scouts of America, Special Olympics Indiana, and Happiness Bag, Inc. His community engagement work as faculty advisor to the Nonprofit Leadership Student Association, Association of Fundraising Professionals Collegiate Chapter, and Autism Speaks U Collegiate Chapter has led him to be recognized as the Indiana State University Outstanding Student Organization Advisor of the Year for three consecutive years. He also serves as a nonprofit management consulting partner for the Indiana Youth Institute. He can be reached at nathan.schaumleffel@indstate.edu.

Dr. Douglas E. Harms, Professor, DePauw University

Douglas Harms is a Professor of Computer Science at DePauw University. In addition to teaching computer science courses he has been involved in encouraging and promoting community engagement at DePauw. He has led a total of six winter-term in-service trips to El Salvador, Mexico, and San Diego where he and his students have studied and learned about social justice, border issues, poverty and homelessness by serving marginalized and at-risk populations. He and his students are also involved with collecting used but usable computers and distributing them to low-income families in the local community. He has been DePauw's faculty liaison to Indiana Campus Compact since 2007, and during 2012–13 and 2013–2014 was an ICC Faculty Fellow. He was a Fulbright Scholar to Bulgaria during the 2004–05 academic year, and was awarded DePauw's G. Bromley Oxnam Award for Service in 2011. He can be reached at dharms@depauw.edu.

Dr. Tina M. Kruger, Assistant Professor, Indiana State University

Tina Kruger is an Assistant Professor in the Department of Applied Health Sciences at Indiana State University. She earned her doctorate in gerontology from the University of Kentucky in 2011 and is now developing a gerontology program at ISU. Community engagement is an important part of Dr. Kruger's teaching activities, her research efforts, and her service on campus and in the community. In addition to serving as an Indiana Campus Compact Faculty Fellow in 2012–2013 and 2013–2014, Dr. Kruger served as co-director of the ISU Science Education through New Civic Engagements and Responsibilities (SENCER) team. She can be reached at tina.krugernewsham@indstate.edu.

Marilyn Lake McElwain, MFA, Instructor, University of Indianapolis

Marilyn Lake McElwain teaches studio and lecture courses in the Department of Art and Design at the University of Indianapolis (UIndy). She received an MFA from the University of Kentucky in

Visual Arts. She has been teaching community engagement courses for ten years both locally and internationally, leading multidisci-
plinary trips to Belize and Greece. While at UIndy, she developed
the Service-learning in the Arts course and a capstone course in
community engagement geared for pre–art therapy majors. She
has received the Indiana Campus Compact Faculty Fellows Award
twice and numerous other grant awards. She is a practicing art-
ist and continues to exhibit two-dimensional works of art as her
schedule allows. She can be reached at mmcelwain@uindy.edu.

Nathan D. Mott, MPA, MS,
Indiana University-Purdue University Indianapolis

Nathan Mott serves as the Indy Learning Centers Director and as
Visiting Research Associate in Purdue School of Engineering and
Technology at Indiana University-Purdue University, Indianapolis.
Nathan established the Indy Learning Centers program in 2007 as
program partners with central Indiana schools to provide tutoring
and academic support for grades two through twelve. He has de-
veloped other projects that relate to service and experiential learn-
ing. Nathan earned his BS and MS in Technology from Purdue
University, Indianapolis, School of Engineering and Technology.
He also completed the MPA in Nonprofit Management from Indiana
University, Indianapolis, School of Public and Environmental
Affairs with a certificate in Social Entrepreneurship. He can be
reached at nmott@iupui.edu.

Dr. Wendy St. Jean, Associate Professor,
Purdue University Calumet

Prof. St. Jean has received degrees from Yale University, the
University of Virginia, and the University of Connecticut. She
has published several articles relating to Native Americans and a
book entitled *Remaining Chickasaw in Indian Territory* (2011). Lately,
she has also been researching the Underground Railroad and

service-learning projects related to the teaching and preservation of historic sites. She can be reached at stjeanw@purduecal.edu.

Indiana Campus Compact Faculty Fellows Staff Liaison
J. R. Jamison, MA, Executive Director,
Indiana Campus Compact

J. R. Jamison is the Executive Director of Indiana Campus Compact and Co-Founder of The Facing Project. Through his role with Indiana Campus Compact, J. R. oversees faculty and professional staff development for member campuses. He is known for coining the phrase *service engagement,* which has been widely used on campuses as a neutralizing bridge builder to begin institutional and community change conversations for campus-community partnerships. Additionally, his framework for building a service engagement infrastructure to support community-based research, teaching, and volunteerism, and his rubric to prepare campuses for institutional planning, have been adopted by more than forty campuses nationwide. He holds a bachelor degree and a Master of Arts in Higher Education Administration from Ball State University. He can be reached at jrjamiso@iupui.edu.

CHAPTER 1:
Why a College and Nonprofit Organization Partnership?

Nathan A. Schaumleffel, PhD, Indiana State University

College and nonprofit partnerships may start in really random ways but can lead to amazing outcomes for both sides. As a brand new faculty member, I was talking with a local business owner and mentioned my interest in aging. He shared that his mother was also interested in aging and that I should get in touch with her. I sent her an e-mail the next day to talk about her work and found out that she was the director of a local nonprofit dedicated to improving health and quality of life for older adults. We've worked on multiple projects together since then and both feel very lucky to have connected.
—Dr. Tina M. Kruger, Dine with a Doc

We all know most nonprofits need more—more people, more supplies, more equipment, more expertise, more space, and more money. This is especially true if we are seriously striving to achieve our organization's mission. Our organizations need these things to impact the people we strive to help. Unfortunately, nonprofit leaders often look right past one of the mother lodes of a community, the local college!

America's colleges have a whole lot of resources that you wish your nonprofit organization (NPO) or nongovernmental organization (NGO) had. Students wish their professors would quit droning on and on in lectures about the real world and how it is going

1

to be someday. Students wish their professors would instead take them out to a local organization and allow them to roll up their sleeves and get real experience doing something meaningful: re-designing a building entrance to be ADA accessible, writing a marketing plan, planning a special event fundraiser, building a website and social media presence, or even creating a volunteer training manual. Colleges can facilitate this connection between students and nonprofits *if* you find the right go-to person or people on your local campus—the movers and shakers, if you will. Find those movers and shakers and the resources may just overfloweth.

Now, the only catch is that if you receiveth you must giveth! You might get that website or marketing plan, but you have to make sure your organization's needs meet the professor's goals for the class project (and that professor might just need a little something for his or her own annual review, too). For partnerships between nonprofits and academics to work, you have to find a way to make your organization's project worth the professor's and students' time, and you might just get an important project done either free of charge or on a shoestring budget.

Now, let me complicate things a bit. Leave it to academic professor-types to complicate everything by splitting hairs over terminology for colleges that have students help out nonprofit organizations. Some terms used by university-types are service-learning, experiential learning, service engagement, internships, volunteer work, practicum, Federal Work-Study student employment, AmeriCorps service, Greek Life, blah, blah, blah, blah, blah. For this book, let's just agree to use the term community engagement when university folks work with a nonprofit to benefit the organization. Community engagement is the broadest term that accurately encompasses all of the ways colleges can provide resources to your organization.

If you would like to view a glossary of hair-splitting terms related to engaging college students in community projects, please view the Glossary of Terms in Appendix A. If you'd like to get started in learning how to access colleges for mission-accomplishing resources—read on.

We hope this book will convince you that it makes good sense to partner with colleges to benefit your organization. Another goal for this book is to better orient you to the scope of services and resources available from colleges. Also, we hope you'll better understand what you and your organization can bring to the table for the students and the professors. We'll coach you on how to get started in seeking out partnerships with colleges; and we'll get into some nitty gritty details about logistics and the legal kind of stuff that you should probably know on the front end. We'll end with ethical issues related to campus-community partnerships.

Good luck in your journey to acquire resources to further your organization's mission by scratching our back and letting us scratch yours.

Resources
Students work to strengthen "Dine with a Doc"
http://www.indstate.edu/news/news.php?newsid=3570

CHAPTER 2:

What is the Value for Nonprofit Organizations Partnering with a College?

Nathan A. Schaumleffel, PhD, Indiana State University

Marilyn Lake McElwain, MFA, University of Indianapolis

Nathan D. Mott, MS, MPA, Indiana University-Purdue University Indianapolis

Our program places college students as tutors in several nonprofit organizations that assist with homework, projects, and test preparation in all academic areas. In particular, our staff is able to offer one-on-one time with tutored students to help them understand concepts that they may not be able to grasp in a traditional classroom setting. The presentation and instruction of material is tailored to students' specific learning styles and needs. Additionally, tutors can explain material based on their students' progress and ability, giving students the chance to truly learn at their own pace.
—Nathan D. Mott, Indy Learning Centers program

Any nonprofit leader—executive director, board president, board member, or volunteer—should carefully weigh the return on investment when expending precious organizational resources in a partnership that may or may not achieve measurable results toward your mission and strategic goals.

Well-governed organizations have a clear and current mission that board members, staff, volunteers, and clients buy into. Moreover, NPOs should have a current, board-developed and approved strategic plan that the executive director is hired to implement by managing the day-to-day operations of the organization.

It is easy for nonprofit leaders to look at the commitment it takes just to be ready to start working toward a mission—an organization has to be created legally, tax-exempt status achieved, board members recruited and trained, a mission and strategic plan developed, funds raised, insurance purchased, and an executive director hired. With that accomplished, the executive director, perhaps you, will sit down the first day on the job and attempt to get settled and to organize the work, hopefully in line with how it will be evaluated.

Nonprofit leaders often start with a board-approved strategic plan that is chock-full of lofty, expensive goals and objectives and has almost no financial or human resources. It can be daunting to think about how to gather the resources, implement programs and services, conduct program evaluation, and confidently document your success toward the mission and strategic goals of the organization, all on a timeline that satisfies the board of directors and meets the urgent needs of your community. Your to-do list of goals and objectives for the strategic plan likely includes starting program evaluation, updating your old website, starting a social media presence, developing a marketing plan, finding funding, or recruiting more volunteers to answer phones and provide basic services.

So much to do and too many places to start, right?

As you develop your priorities and organize your work, think about the people and money that it will take to make it all happen. For instance, if your plan is to have a better website, it is going to take people to put this plan into action as well as money for web hosting, e-mail accounts, and the like.

As a leader, you know you're going to need help putting your plan into action, however, all of your staff and volunteers are already swamped with the daily duties that keep the organization's doors open and operating. Or you may feel you have some great staff members, but they lack the technical skills to put the plan into action. So what do you do? Call up some friends and ask if they know anyone? Beg someone who is already too busy with his or her six other board positions to join your board? Call your alma mater to see if your college professor has any ideas? You may even post a newly created position online, or hire an independent contractor or consultant to provide services.

Nonprofits generally invest heavily in human resources, that is, paid part-time or full-time staff and volunteers. For most nonprofits, people are the most important asset to achieving the mission. Unfortunately, paid staffing (i.e., salaries, payroll taxes, health insurance, paid vacation, maternity leave, etc.) often costs an organization up to 70 percent of its monthly operating expenses.

By now, you may be thinking about cloning yourself, or simply never sleeping again, but ultimately your job is to work smart and hard. One of the most critical functions of a nonprofit executive director, or a board president of an organization that has no paid executive director, is the ability to build relationships and develop resources through fundraising, volunteer management, and in-kind donations of equipment and supplies. This is exactly where colleges can be valuable partners for your organization—if you can figure out how to get in and connected with the right people.

Most colleges have multifaceted missions. For example, colleges are not solely tasked with educating students. They must also prepare students to be competitive in the job market and to be active citizens (which means more than voting every four years and includes being active volunteers, donors, and board members to nonprofit organizations). Colleges are increasingly using community engagement projects to educate students.

Community engagement projects that bring value to your organization often tie into a variety of college courses from nonprofit management to gerontology, to computer science, to business, to marketing, to history, to social work, to law enforcement, to nursing and therapeutic professions, to the fine, performing, and studio arts, and beyond! Depending on the mission of the organization, or the function of the agency, college faculty and students utilize their skills in accounting, computer graphic design, tutoring, after-school programming, music lessons, painting, cosmetology, grounds beautification, tax preparation, and veterans assistance to name a few. Students have painted murals, taught art and music classes, created after-school programs, overseen theatrical performances, and led therapeutic horseback riding lessons.

Valuable projects and resources may also include, but are not limited to, the following:

- Needs assessments (e.g., needs of parents of children with autism spectrum disorder, survey design, data collection, coding, entry, analysis, reporting)

- Training/workshop development (e.g., new government regulations—Medicaid Part D, Obamacare, PF-990 filing)

- Asset mapping

- Strategic planning

- Marketing plans

- Graphic design

- Website design and maintenance

- Mission-focused program, service, event planning and leadership (e.g., health education, tutoring, invasive species removal, historical interpretation services for museums, tax preparation, tutoring, music lessons, coaching, care of injured sea turtles, organization of clothing and food drives, work in international settings helping a Mayan pottery co-op solve pottery glazing issues)

- Fundraising campaigns (e.g., direct mail, direct e-mail, phone solicitation, donor management, prospecting)

- Grant proposal writing

- Program evaluation and logic modeling

- Media campaigns

- Facility safety assessment

- Facility and site design (e.g., park design, engineering projects)

- Board development

- Volunteer management (e.g., criminal background screening, recognition program)

- Staff and volunteer training and manuals

- Landscape architecture (e.g., grounds beautification)

- Accounting and budgeting

- Legal counsel

- Nonnative language (e.g., translation of health brochures, preparation of taxes for non-English speaking populations, teaching English as a second language)

- Equipment and supplies procurement (e.g., teaching supplies, art supplies, construction materials, software, snacks for children in after-school programs, clothing, sports equipment, landscaping materials, books, and various other staples)

Community engagement projects for colleges take the form of projects that meet multiple goals for multiple stakeholders: (1) your organization, (2) the students, and (3) the faculty member. The basic design for community engagement projects is mixed as they are not just for student learning. They are also not just for your organization to get something free of charge that you couldn't otherwise afford. Their purpose is both and then some! Projects must be well designed so that all parties get a satisfactory return on investment of time and resources. Think of a Venn diagram of overlapping priorities. The shaded part in the middle is service engagement. Faculty have the role and responsibility to ensure that students can demonstrate course learning outcomes and that they achieve the deliverables to your organization. So, if you're working with a writing class to review content on your website, understand that the project is not just about your website. The faculty member will also work with you as a community partner to ensure the experience is more than an academic exercise for students and that your valuable time and resources are not wasted. Faculty have the responsibility of balancing appropriate student learning and assessment while ensuring you get what you need. They also have to make sure they get what they need for their own investment of time and resources—more on faculty serving at their risk later.

Community engagement is a juggling of multiple, yet equally important, priorities.

Additionally, college and community partnerships can bring value to a nonprofit organization through the following:

- Energizing the organization's personnel, volunteers, and programs

- Providing new ways of looking at old things

- Funding programs they could not normally provide

- Giving new visibility that often attracts donors and additional community support

- Promoting diversity and cultural competence among nonprofit program participants by bringing college students from other cultures into local nonprofits to interact with program participants

- Supporting the work as being valuable because it has received validation from others

As you can see, there are scores of ways that colleges can bring value to a nonprofit organization through a community engagement partnership, but please understand that nonprofits bring immense value to colleges as well. The relationship is a partnership, not a one way street where the college is acting as savior for local nonprofits and downtrodden people. Nonprofits make it possible for colleges to meet their educational missions and goals also, which means nonprofits and colleges need to be viewed as equal partners helping each other. More on what colleges get out of these partnerships in chapter 5.

References

Bloom, B. S., ed. *Taxonomy of Educational Objectives: The Classification of Educational Goals, handbook I, cognitive domain.* (New York: Longmans, Green, 1956).

CHAPTER 3:

What College Partners Can Offer Nonprofit Organizations: Time, Treasure, and Talent

Nathan A. Schaumleffel, PhD, Indiana State University

Marilyn Lake McElwain, MFA, University of Indianapolis

Students in the university's Nonprofit Leadership Alliance program worked with nine ScoutReach Cub Scout packs in the Terre Haute, Indiana area to evaluate the effectiveness of the Scouting program. By using scientific research methods, the evaluation team determined that the ScoutReach program is positively impacting Scouts' lifestyle behaviors. The partnership with the ISU-NLA chapter and my district ScoutReach team has been an amazing opportunity to really do an in-depth evaluation of our program's effectiveness. Budgetary constraints prevent most nonprofits from being able to undertake such a venture, but thanks to these cooperative efforts, we are well along the path of making our program even stronger and more effective for the youth of the Wabash Valley.
—Tony Doyle, District ScoutReach Specialist

We all know most nonprofits need more—more people, more supplies, more equipment, more expertise, more space, and more money, especially if we are seriously striving to achieve our organization's mission in measurable ways. Unfortunately, even when a nonprofit organization needs more, nonprofit leaders often look right past one of the mother lodes of a community and do not include it in the organization's asset map, the local college! America's colleges can provide the time, treasure, and talent to assist your organization—if you find the right go-to person or people on your local campus....the movers and shakers if you will. Find the movers and shakers and the resources may just overfloweth.

Before seeking out the movers and shakers at a college to channel time, treasure, and talent to your organization, you and your organization need to do some critical strategic planning. You shouldn't put the cart before the horse by approaching a college for time, treasure, and talent, if your organization does not have an organized and trained board with a functional strategic plan (Schaumleffel 2014a). After you have completed the planning process discussed below, then you can start establishing relationships and partnerships with faculty and staff from a college and begin the work toward community engagement projects.

This chapter will first provide a brief overview of nonprofit organizational strategic planning, which includes SWOT (strengths, weaknesses, opportunities, and threats) analysis, asset mapping, needs assessments, goal setting, and program development. The goal of this section is to help nonprofit executives, board members, and volunteers understand the critical role of strategic planning, so that they can be knowledgeable not only about what they need from a college-community partnership but also what they can bring to the table. This information is presented here as a light orientation to strategic planning in order to frame the rest of the chapter. The bulk of this chapter will then comprehensively outline the time, treasure, and talent to be garnered from a college. So let's get started...

Strategic Planning, Asset Mapping, Needs Assessments, Goal Setting, and Program Development

As previously mentioned, nonprofit organizations need trained board members who function well together as a group. Why does a nonprofit organization need a trained board of directors with a strategic plan? Most nonprofit leaders need, or think they need, more resources. Unfortunately, the less mission focused an organization is, the more resources the organization's board, staff, and volunteers seem to think they need, because they are offering a vast array of programs, services, and events that are not necessarily aligned with their mission statement, goals, and objectives. This causes mission drift and can waste valuable human and financial resources on programs and services that do not make a measurable impact on the target audience (Schaumleffel 2014a). So the question becomes, how does your organization improve so that it operates the way it ought to (Schaumleffel 2014a)?

First, to operate an efficient and impactful, mission-focused nonprofit organization, your board needs to be trained in how to work as a group and each person needs to be trained in how to be an effective individual board member. Once this training is accomplished, the board of directors needs to make the mission statement the roots or rock of the organization—the prism through which all decisions are made (Schaumleffel 2014a). The board needs to revisit the organization's mission statement annually and affirm it, revise it, or change it (Schaumleffel 2014a). Once the mission statement is set, the board needs to embark on a strategic planning process that proceeds to mapping organizational assets, and is driven by a needs assessment of the target audience to be served (Schaumleffel 2014a).

Before contacting a college or faculty member, and before embarking on a needs assessment, it is important to conduct a SWOT analysis and then organizational asset mapping as part of your strategic planning.

SWOT Analysis

SWOT analysis is a strategic planning tactic often used by nonprofit leaders. The SWOT acronym stands for Strengths, Weaknesses, Opportunities, and Threats. Through this process, insight is gained into the organization's assets from the strengths and opportunities analyses. When an organization scrutinizes its needs and weaknesses, leaders can consider ways to minimize mission drift and often correct issues that are not normally seen as a positive aspect of a program or service. The final area to analyze is that of potential or real threats. By using the SWOT analysis, along with a follow-up discussion, detecting potential threats or challenges may present new opportunities in the making. Depending on how these potential issues are handled, positive outcomes may result, and new assets or strengths may develop. SWOT analysis is a critical prestep to asset mapping.

Asset Mapping

"Community asset mapping is a needs assessment technique that involves the process of intentionally identifying the human, material, financial, entrepreneurial and other resources in a community" (Eisenhauer, Marthakis, Jamison, & Mattson. 2011, 168). Many of the assets listed may come from the strengths and opportunities sections of your SWOT analysis. The college faculty or staff member that you partner with will want to know ahead of time what the nonprofit agency has to offer for the project. Be specific in listing all assets that are available in the community for the project, including potential assets that the local college can provide. Consider both physical and financial resources that can be allocated for the collaboration. What can the college partner expect from the agency in terms of accessible spaces, equipment, supplies, personnel, or even funds that may supplement the resources that they provide for the collaboration? Your organizational asset map will come in handy when negotiating a college-community partnership, because it will bring clarity to the internal assets that your organization can bring to the table for a college-community partnership, as well as the external assets that the college may bring to the table. Once assets are mapped by the nonprofit organization, it is time to look at the next step of strategic planning, which is to conduct the needs assessment.

Needs Assessment

What is a needs assessment? Needs assessment is a "systematic process to determine and document a community's or a community organization's needs" (Eisenhauer et al. 2011, 170). While the National Service-Learning Clearing House Fact Sheet (2011) states that a needs assessment "is a tool for program planning that helps determine "what a community already has, what it wants or needs, and what it hopes." Although planning and implementing a needs assessment is a critical function of any nonprofit organization in establishing or revising its mission statement and strategic plan, as well as devising its programs and services, many, if not the vast majority, of NPOs struggle terribly with conducting a reliable and valid needs assessment process. In fact, one of the greatest talents an NPO can commandeer from a college through a partnership is simply getting help with assessing needs, from developing questionnaires and leading focus groups to coding, inputting, analyzing, interpreting, and reporting data.

Before embarking on a needs-assessment project, a nonprofit organization needs to determine what information they need to make the necessary strategic planning decisions for program and service delivery. Once the type of information needed is deciphered, then the organization should seek out existing, secondary data before deciding to collect its own primary data through an in-house survey. Nonprofits can gather existing data from a variety of sources. For example, government agencies such as the US Census Bureau, and independent organizations like the Indiana Youth Institute that publishes an annual Kids Count Data Book regarding statistics on youth in the State of Indiana (http://www.iyi.org/reports.aspx).

Needs assessments are typically designed as a survey or questionnaire and administered with paper and pencil or, more often, as an e-survey using e-mail and an online survey service like SurveyMonkey. Needs assessments can also take the form of interviews, focus groups, and community meetings. Regardless of the data-collection method, the goal is to gather input primarily from the target audience to be served, such as clients, participants, users, or customers. Data are also gathered from other internal stakeholders such as volunteers, part-time staff, full-time staff, and board members, as well as external stakeholders.

For example, a school may have a population of students who could benefit from after-school tutoring. In this case, a needs assessment could be useful. A survey could be designed and implemented that would gather input from students, parents or guardians, teachers, and administrators. The first questions may address the type of after-school program most beneficial to the designated student population. In other words, what types of issues are the students having? The survey could be designed to determine what supplies are needed to carry out the program. Is space available for such an after-school program? Is after-school transportation available to students? In terms of the college partners, how often will college students be available for tutoring, and will they have their own transportation? Are college-student tutors proficient in the areas that have been determined as most crucial for the tutoring program?

Once needs are determined, the organization, under the leadership of the board of directors and the professional expertise of the executive director, can finalize the organization's strategic plan by developing measurable goals, objectives, strategies, and tasks that include time frames, timetables, and deadlines (Schaumleffel 2014a). Ultimately, goals and objectives become programs, services, and events aimed at serving the organization's target audience in order to achieve the mission statement (Schaumleffel 2014a).

Establishing Goals, Objectives, Strategies, and Tasks that Connect to Program Development Logic Modeling

The goals, objectives, strategies, and tasks developed in the strategic plan must be based on the needs assessment findings and include program, service, and event plans that are aligned with the mission statement (Schaumleffel 2014a). Current programs that are not aligned with the mission, that is have drifted from the mission, should be responsibly ended (Schaumleffel 2014a). New mission-focused programs, services, and events should be structured with a program evaluation plan that includes a logic model with strategies, activities, and necessary resources (Schaumleffel 2014a).

Many nonprofit leaders do not understand or simply do not partake in the mission-focused planning process as outlined above (Schaumleffel 2014a). Do-gooders want to do good right now, not systematically plan first (Schaumleffel 2014a). You see, the needs assessment in the strategic planning process leads to the list of resources needed in the program evaluation logic model, which ultimately leads to the list of things you need to receive from a local college through a college-community partnership.

A college-community partnership should then be strategic, with a high probability for strong return on investments (ROI) based on the organization's mission, strategic plan, measurable goals and objectives, and program evaluation logic models. Mutually beneficial partnerships will meet the needs of all individuals and organizations in the partnership. In the case of college and community partnerships, the partnerships will meet the needs of the organization; the organization's clients, staff, and volunteers; the students; and the faculty.

Petzoldt's Mantra: Know What You Know,
Know What You Don't Know

All in all, nonprofit organizations require capacity, know-how, and professional leadership and management. A good heart to do good and a desire to volunteer and serve are simply not enough to lead and manage a mission-focused organization that does things the way they oughta be done in a sustainable, perpetual way (Schaumleffel 2014a). If you or your organization is struggling with the topics discussed thus far in this chapter, you should strongly consider investing in training and consulting services. If the local college has a nonprofit leadership and management expert, you may contact him or her for expertise, training, and consulting. Otherwise, you should consider getting training and consulting services from independent consultants, or from organizations like the Indiana Youth Institute (http://www.iyi.org/consulting-servic-es.aspx), or the Indiana Nonprofit Resource Network (http://www. inrn.org/). By working with a consultant, you'll be able to take that do-good spirit and actually make an impact on the people you want to help!

Garnering Time, Treasure, and Talent from a Local College

So, where would a nonprofit executive, board president, or volunteer look on a college campus to turn on the faucet of resources? That is a good question! Well, let's just take a look at all of the rocks you should consider looking under. This chapter is not intended to be exhaustive for every campus. Its purpose is simply to paint a much broader picture of what actually is available on college campuses—resources that could easily benefit your organization in terms of achieving the measurable goals and objectives from your strategic plan that are aligned with your mission statement.

The first thing to do is simply invoke the power of Google. Google the college campus closest to your organization. Once you land on the campus's website (usually ending in .edu), use the site's search function to find the following units, divisions, or departments on campus: Center for Community Engagement, Sponsored Programs, Grants and Contracts, Distance Education, Nonprofit Leadership, Career Center, etc. They might even have a Search A–Z function on their website, which may prove helpful.

You'll need to find a way to make at least one new friend in each of these units, divisions, or departments by utilizing the on-campus and community networking addressed at the end of this chapter. As you find each unit, division, or department listed below, you should spend time reading the faculty and staff biographies to learn about these folks' experience, interests, and involvement. Many of them may already have volunteered for your organization! Many can serve in a variety of short- and long-term volunteer roles for your organization, also. Some will volunteer for one day, others may serve on your board of directors for years. Many will serve in a regular nonboard role for years if you engage them with your volunteer management skills. Most university employees are well educated, but they are often strapped with student loan debt and not all that well paid for their education and experience, so you should engage these folks for time and talent, and not necessarily target them for treasure (beyond a $100 or less annual fund gift). University personnel make excellent advisory committee members (at a level above a casual volunteer but not on the board of directors).

Center for Community Engagement or Center for Service-Learning

A great starting point is the Center for Community Engagement or Center for Service-Learning. Many campuses have created these offices as their front door to the community. These offices often have funding opportunities as well as affiliated faculty. Their staff tends to know many, but not all, of the movers and shakers on campus. Often these offices also host volunteer fairs,

United Way Days of Service, MLK Days of Service, and Alternative Fall and Spring Breaks. If your office is close to campus, it is not uncommon for a nonprofit to serve as a host site for the myriad days of service. At these days of service, scores of college students will visit your organization for a few hours to a full day to clean, paint, and fix up your facility inside and out. These service days are a great way to showcase your agency to potential long-term volunteers.

Many college campuses have created formal volunteer corps and have created volunteer transcripts or cocurricular transcripts for students. It will be important to your organization to know if your local college campus offers this documentation for students and, if so, market your organization's volunteer opportunities to students for improving their volunteer or cocurricular transcript.

Also, most Centers for Community Engagement and Centers for Service-Learning have a Community Council made up of local nonprofit leaders. You'll want to get a seat on this council and participate actively. Participation on campus committees like these typically provides a great return on investment for your time (and ensuring good return on investment is an important quality when choosing to spread yourself thinner).

You should also consider making it a habit to provide and educate the staff of the Center for Community Engagement or Center for Service-Learning on these characteristics of your organization: mission, strategic plan with specific goals and objectives, needs, and available resources. This will keep your organization's needs at the forefront of staff awareness, and prepare the faculty, academic staff, and your own organization for a variety of community engagement projects. Staff members can recommend campus movers and shakers who may be a good match for you, as well as highlight your organization's needs at Center for Community Engagement affiliated faculty and staff meetings.

Office of Sponsored Programs and/or Office of Grants and Contracts

The Office of Sponsored Programs, albeit a strange name, is often the name of the campus office that assists faculty and staff with grant opportunity searching, grant proposal and budget preparation, and grant proposal submission. The experts that staff the sponsored programs office have excellent technical expertise, as well as access to grant databases that are fee or subscription based, which small and medium-sized nonprofit organizations typically can't afford to access. Most sponsored programs offices cannot afford the time to assist all nonprofits in a campus community with grant funding, so it's helpful to make a campus friend who can get your foot in the door. Many college campuses are marketing themselves as engaged or community-involved campuses, which means they will help community agencies when possible. The secret to gaining access to a college office of sponsored programs is to find a way to connect your program or project to the work of a faculty member. Then you will be able to access this office via the faculty or staff member. If your faculty colleague is savvy, they can ethically engage the sponsored programs staff on your organization's funding needs.

AmeriCorps

AmeriCorps, often described as the domestic Peace Corps, is a federally funded program administered by the National Corporation for Community Service that places people in a variety of approved nonprofit sites. Many colleges facilitate student placement at nonprofits for AmeriCorps. It is fairly simple to work with your local AmeriCorps provider to have your agency established as an AmeriCorps-approved site. AmeriCorps staff will serve at your organization for anywhere from three hundred service hours to nearly seven hundred hours of service, and they will essentially function as staff for your organization. Students can serve at your agency as an AmeriCorps staffer unattached to a class or for academic credit. However, it often works well to combine an AmeriCorps appointment with a for-credit internship experience if you can find the right faculty member who can make it work for the student, the college AmeriCorps coordinator, and your organization.

Federal Work-Study

When most people think of student employment jobs on a college campus, especially those designated as Federal Work-Study (FWS) positions, they tend to think of students working in Residential Life Dining Hall positions serving sloppy joes, washing dishes, reloading the Lucky Charms dispenser, shuffling campus mail around a building, or serving as an administrative aide to a campus office. What most nonprofit folks do not realize is that colleges can designate student employment Federal Work-Study positions to be served at your agency for community-service positions. In fact, by federal law, 7 percent of a college's FWS federal allocation for an award year must be used for community-service positions (US Department of Education, Federal Student Aid (USDOE-FSA) n.d.). That's right—a college must assign some of its student employees who are funded via Federal Work-Study to nonprofit organizations. In short, the student works for your organization, but they get paid as a student employee of the university.

Typically, Federal Work-Study dollars will cover 75 percent of the student's hourly pay and the nonprofit organization covers 25 percent (USDOE-FSA n.d.). In some cases, a nonprofit may get 90 percent of a student's hourly wage paid by FWS, while in other cases a student employee working on family literacy issues in a nonprofit organization may qualify for 100 percent of his or her wage to be covered by FWS (USDOE-FSA n.d.). Some preference is also given to math and reading tutors.

Typically, Federal Work-Study programs are administered on a college campus via the Student Financial Aid Department, since FWS positions for students are based on need as established via the financial aid process by the federal government. In addition, the student employee must enroll in at least one credit hour, demonstrate financial need, and work part time (USDOE-FSA, n.d.). Wages are subject to federal IRS withholdings and are included in the student's financial aid package (USDOE-FSA n.d.).

You also might locate this resource on a campus by contacting student employment, human resources, or the campus career center offices. To learn more about Federal Work-Study opportunities for your organization, read the US Department of Education's training guide, the *2013–2014 Federal Student Aid Handbook*:

http://ifap.ed.gov/fsahandbook/attachments/1314FSA HbkVol6Ch2.pdf

Student Activities and Organizations
Almost every college has a mechanism for students to create approved, official student clubs and organizations. Some are cultural, others recreational, some even preprofessional, service, or honor societies. Almost all student clubs encourage their members to engage in service and philanthropy. These clubs are often called RSOs (i.e., registered student organizations) and are typically managed by the university through the division of student affairs. Most universities' fiscal policies allow RSOs to make monetary donations to your organization from their fundraising initiatives. Moreover, some of America's best-known nonprofit organizations, such as Girl Scouts USA, have affiliated campus RSOs called Campus Girl Scouts.

http://en.wikipedia.org/wiki/Membership_levels_of_the_ Girl_Scouts_of_the_USA#Campus_Girl_Scouts

http://www.indiana.edu/~girlsct/

Autism Speaks has a system of Autism Speaks U (http://events.autismspeaks.org/site/c.nuLTJ6MPKrH/b.8760443/k.BDB5/Home.htm) collegiate chapters scattered around the country. As noted in the following article, this programming is growing quickly.

Students fight autism, gain experience working for nonprofit agency

http://www.indstate.edu/news/news.php?newsid=2905

Unfortunately, it is not always the case that the local affiliate of a national organization even knows that a campus-affiliated RSO exists at the college campus in the same community. Some other organizations like the American Cancer Society have collegiate Relay for Life chapters in the form of RSOs (http://college.relayforlife.org/getinvolved/collegesagainstcancer/), as well as St. Jude Children's Research Hospital has collegiate Up 'Til Dawn chapters (http://fundraising.stjude.org/site/PageServer?pagename=utd_home) and Riley Hospital for Children in Indianapolis has collegiate Dance Marathon fundraising collegiate chapters (http://www.rileykids.org/events/dance_marathons/host_an_event/). Best Buddies (http://www.bestbuddies.org/our-programs), Kiwanis (Circle K) International (http://www.circlek.org/home.aspx), and TOMS shoes (http://www.tomscommunity.com/TOMSCampusClubs) all have collegiate chapter programs.

College campuses are also flush with faith-based RSOs that have scores of caring, service-oriented members, for example, Christian Student Fellowship, United Campus Ministries, Campus Outreach, Adventist Student Fellowship, Baptist Student Ministry, Chi Alpha Campus Ministries, Divine Praise, Fellowship of Christian Athletes, Interfaith Fellowship, InterVarsity Christian Fellowship, Islamic Society of Ahl-ul-Bayt, Journey Campus Ministry, Latter-Day Saints Student Association, Lutheran Student Fellowship, Muslim Students Association, and Orthodox Christian Fellowship.

Also, campus recreation centers tend to oversee Recreational-Sport Clubs, such as rugby, wrestling, martial arts, ultimate Frisbee, fishing, fencing, ballroom dance, rodeo, and baseball to name a few. These RSOs, if approached by the right nonprofit organization, can provide amazing resources to a local nonprofit.

Preprofessional (i.e., Major-Related) Organizations and Honor Societies

Besides the RSOs mentioned above, several RSOs affiliated with student activities and organizations are categorized as preprofessional organizations. Some of these organizations are tied to a particular major, while others are attached to a major and to a national or international professional organization. Examples of preprofessional campus organizations that nonprofit executives may want to establish a relationship with include the Student Social Work Association, the Association of Fundraising Professionals collegiate chapter (http://www.afpnet.org/Audiences/ChapterNewsDetail. cfm?ItemNumber=2575), American Association of Family and Consumer Sciences student club, American Marketing Association student club, Construction Club, and the Nonprofit Leadership Student Association.

Preprofessional organizations related to philanthropy, service, and nonprofit management create amazing partnerships that train students, build their resumes, and assist your organization. For example, some nonprofit leadership student organizations conduct projects with local nonprofit organizations, such as those described in the following articles:

- Nonprofit Leadership Students Evaluate Wabash Valley Cub Scout Programs http://www.indstate.edu/news/news. php?newsid=3448

- Tie Between University, Special Olympics Continues to Grow http://www.indstate.edu/news/news.php?newsid=3375

- Nonprofit Leadership Students Contribute to Health Organizations
  http://www.indstate.edu/news/news.php?newsid=3049

- ISU Students Provide Fun, Educational Programming with Venture Crew http://www.tribstar.com/schools/x744037017/ISU-students-provide-fun-educational-programming-with-Venture-Crew

- Y Program to Feed Hungry, Get You Healthy
  http://www.tribstar.com/news/x964877868/Y-program-to-feed-hungry-get-you-healthy

- Indiana State to Celebrate Earth Day April 21
  http://www.indstate.edu/news/news.php?newsid=2700

- Students Sponsor Goodwill Drive
  http://www.indstate.edu/news/isutoday.php?articleid=2372

- Students to Gain Fundraising Training, Opportunities through New Organization
  http://www.indstate.edu/news/news.php?newsid=1994

- ISU Students Host Ducks on the Wabash
  http://www.mywabashvalley.com/story/isu-students-host-ducks-on-the-wabash/d/story/xKAqBldvDUWq_eu2YdRV9Q

There are also a variety of academic honor societies that are often tied to a specific academic department or major. These organizations serve as an academic honor society, as well as a preprofessional group and sometimes as a service organization also. These organizations often have Greek names, such as those for social and service fraternities and sororities, and are often called fraternities. They tend to be coed and are often connected to a national professional association such as the following:

- Rho Phi Lambda, the National Honorary Recreation, Park, and Leisure Services (coed) fraternity (connected with the National Recreation and Park Association) http://rhophilambda.org/

- Eta Sigma Rho, the National Health Education Honorary http://etasigmagamma.org/

- Phi Kappa Phi, an honor society for all disciplines http://www.phikappaphi.org/web/

Service and Advocacy Organizations
Besides the preprofessional organizations listed above, colleges often also have a number of service-oriented RSOs such as Alpha Phi Omega (http://www.apo.org/Home), originally a service-fraternity only for Eagle Scouts. APO is now a campus-based coed service-fraternity that subscribes to Scouting values at over three hundred and fifty colleges, but it's open for membership to any college student whether they have a Scouting background or not.

There are other RSOs that provide service to the community and advocate for the improvement of the human condition and for society through collegiate chapters, such as the NAACP Youth and College Division (http://www.naacp.org/programs/entry/youth-and-college) and Amnesty International (http://www.amnestyusa.org/resources/students-and-youth).

Greek Life: Social Fraternities and Sororities
Greek organizations, social fraternities, and sororities are another version of RSOs as described above. However, they often have

stricter, more active, and more robust service requirements, as well as an organized philanthropy program. Most national fraternity and sorority organizations have a targeted philanthropic partner for which their local collegiate chapters serve and raise money. For example, the Gamma Phi Beta (http://www.gammaphibeta.org/foundation/givetoyourpassion) sorority's national philanthropy is Camp Fire (formerly Camp Fire USA, Camp Fire Boys and Girls, and Camp Fire Girls) (http://www.campfireusa.org/cfGPB.aspx). If you are a local affiliate (i.e., council) of Camp Fire, you can simply go to Gamma Phi Beta's national website, search for the collegiate chapter closest to your council, and strike up a service and philanthropic partnership that will benefit your organization as well as help the sorority members develop their service engagement ethic.

Nonprofit leaders should embrace the opportunity to work with social fraternities and sororities on local college campuses. These modern day Greeks are not the stereotypical Belushi-era partiers of yesteryear. Greek Life organizations can provide valuable time, treasure, and talent to your organization in an extremely professional manner.

Academic Affairs: Traditional and Nontraditional Disciplines
Many nonprofit leaders do not understand the scope and relevance to nonprofits of many of the degrees and disciplines being offered in America's colleges today. Many colleges are offering the following majors, minors, certificates, and graduate degrees that directly prepare students for the nonprofit sector or simply compliment the nonprofit sector:

- Adult Education and Training

- Athletic Training/Sports Medicine

- Business

- Communication

- Community Development/Community Organizing

- Community Psychology

- Educational Administration

- Gerontology

- Health Administration

- Higher Education

- Human Development and Family Studies

- Human Resource Development

- Leadership Studies

- Management

- Marketing

- Nonprofit Leadership and Management

- Philanthropy

- Psychology

- Public Administration

- Public Policy

- Public Relations

- Public/Community Health

- Recreation Management

- Rural Sociology

- Social Entrepreneurship

- Social Work

- Sociology

- Sport Management

- Student Affairs

- Youth Leadership/Youth Development/Youth Work

After reviewing this list, you'll quickly see that almost every major has relevance to the nonprofit sector. It could be a philosophy major serving a nonprofit faith-based organization, a political science major serving a nonprofit political action committee, a construction management major serving a nonprofit labor union, a theater major serving a nonprofit community theater, a health administration major serving a nonprofit health clinic or hospital foundation, a language studies major serving an international nongovernmental organization, or a business major creating a social enterprise.

Partnering with units in Academic Affairs will tend to be course-based projects, internships, volunteer work, practicum hours, observations, field work, or service-learning. The following describe examples:

- Autism Speaks—Leading the Way: Autism-Friendly Youth Organizations
  http://www.autismspeaks.org/family-services/youth-organizations

- Students Work to Strengthen "Dine with a Doc"
  http://www.indstate.edu/news/news.php?newsid=3570

- Nonprofit Leadership Students Evaluate Wabash Valley Cub Scout Programs
  http://www.indstate.edu/news/news.php?newsid=3448

- Tie Between University, Special Olympics Continues to Grow
  http://www.indstate.edu/news/news.php?newsid=3375

- ISU Recognized for Nonprofit Education (Wins National Nonprofit Leadership Alliance—2013 Sprint Campus Partner of the Year Award)
  http://www.insideindianabusiness.com/newsitem.asp?ID=58055

- ISU Nonprofit Leadership Alliance–Sprint Campus of the Year Nomination video:
  http://www.youtube.com/watch?v=sojs5Eezc1E&list=UU2Z2qkLfYt_ilLkK23T8xxA&index=4

- Service-Learning Project Aims to Make Exercise Fun
  http://www.indstate.edu/news/news.php?newsid=1782

- ISU Students Assist in Creating a Master Plan for Clay City
  http://www.thebraziltimes.com/story/1461854.html

- Clay City has a Plan, Thanks to ISU Prof and Students
http://www.indstate.edu/news/news.php?newsid=1433

- Reaching Out to Rural Indiana: ISU Students Help Create
Plan for Clay City http://www.tribstar.com/features/
x681803995/Reaching-out-to-rural-Indiana-ISU-students-
help-create-plan-for-Clay-City?keyword=topstory

- Rural Recreation Development in Clay City (video) mms://
wms.indstate.edu/cmvp/2007/inrrdp-students.wmv

- Rural Recreation Development Training for State of Indiana
(video 1) mms://wms.indstate.edu/cmvp/2007/wtwo-inrrdp.
wmv
http://www.tribstar.com/local/x1155772798/Rural-
Recreation-Development-Training-session-set-for-Oct-23

- Rural Recreation Development Training for State of Indiana
(video 2)
mms://wms.indstate.edu/cmvp/2007/inrrdp-conference.wmv

- Agritourism Could be Boon to Rural Indiana Communities
http://www.indstate.edu/inrrdp/docs/clay-city/clay-city-ag.pdf

Career Center

Most colleges have invested resources in a campus career center
to serve as a catalyst to transition students from being students
to employed professionals. Career center services tend to include
career exploration and planning, resume and interviewing coaching, campus career fairs, networking training, etiquette dinners,
internship and externship programs, and job searching assistance.
Career centers tend to partner with the college's alumni association to coordinate alumni hiring their own. Nonprofit organizations can engage with career centers by offering to serve as an

internship or externship site, exhibit at career fairs, and serve as professional mentors to students.

Residential Life

What many might think of as dorms are actually highly engaged living-learning communities that can benefit your organization in a variety of ways! In today's residence halls, dorm is nothing more than a four-letter word...and not in a good way. Residential life staff, as well as all staff and academic professionals throughout student affairs, are educators first, and they are just as important to student learning and development (if not more so) than those pesky professors. The Residential Life experience is a dynamic learning laboratory for leadership, group dynamics, service, community, diversity, respect, and interpersonal skills—in other words, all of the things necessary for nonprofits to be successful. Residential Life on college campuses tends to have a Residence Hall Association (RHA), sort of like a student council made up of representatives from individual floors and halls. The representatives tend to be residents, not resident assistants (RAs). Typically, each hall has its own council also. Most of the time, RHA and each individual hall council have an academic year budget to spend on programs, events, facility improvements, and, many times, philanthropy.

Residence halls are not the dorms that you or your parents knew in the 1950s, 1960s, 1970s, 1980s, and 1990s. The open showers and bathroom stalls with no doors are being phased out quickly to give schools a competitive edge in student recruitment. Phone booths and TV-watching rooms are gone, too. Resident hall facilities are being designed to facilitate student learning, community building, and service.

Residential Life is partnering with folks in Academic Affairs to create themed housing by major, minors, or by issue. For example, some campuses have specific floors or halls entirely set aside for those majoring in nursing, aviation, or even nonprofit leadership.

Other campuses have themed housing centered around interdisciplinary and interprofessional issues and social issues, such as hunger, poverty, sustainability, or disease prevention. Depending on the mission of your organization, you may be able to create a partnership with Residential Life's themed housing that ties to a relevant academic major, as well as the academic department that administers the academic program. For example, if your organization is the Friends of Shakamak State Park, you might seek out Residential Life staff who can grant you access to the conservation minors residence hall, or to the interdisciplinary themed housing that rallies around the issue of sustainability.

Residential Life typically requires RAs to plan and implement a variety of programs throughout the academic year in a variety of domains that promote holistic human development, career development, and healthy living. It is a good strategy to make friends with Residential Life administrators. Become a regular, as a local nonprofit leader, on the floor programming-circuit in order to promote your organization. You should strive to become known as an easy program to coordinate for an RA, one that they can count on to have good attendance by their residents. Some colleges, such as Southern Illinois University Carbondale, go as far as recruiting faculty and staff to serve as Faculty and Staff Associates that serve as mentors to the residents and a confidant to the RA for an academic year. A Faculty and Staff Associate is usually assigned to one RA and his or her residents. Innovative campuses are creating the same opportunity for community members. You may find working into this role on a nearby college campus has a good return on investment for your organization.

Student Government

Nearly every college campus has some form of student government. Student governments are typically designed after the American representative democracy with legislative, executive, and judicial branches. Student governments are often tasked with serving as grant makers to student organizations on their campuses. Most importantly, student government can be a critical communication conduit to the entire campus regarding the needs of your organization, and student government can serve as a referral agent or matchmaker to connect your organization with the right group of students on campus. To access student government and the marketing power of student government, you'll need to understand the structure of most student governments, so that you can navigate to the correct people to help you.

Typically, in the executive branch under the leadership of the student government president is a student director of campus life. Also, in the legislative branch within the student senate, there is typically a senate committee called the campus life committee. In theory, the senate campus life committee and the executive branch's student director of campus life work together in concert under the supervision of a full-time academic professional employee. This employee is often called the coordinator or director of student organizations.

The last thing you should know is that some of the most engaged students are in student government, as well as in multiple other student leadership roles on campus. In short, your job is to find the movers and shakers on-campus. Student government is a fantastic way to do just that, as described in the following:

- Five Receive Hines Medal for Academic Achievement
  http://www.indstate.edu/news/news.php?newsid=3543

- Alumni, Student Speakers Announce for Spring Commencement
  http://www.indstate.edu/news/news.php?newsid=3538

- Five Grads Receive Hines Medal
  http://www.indstate.edu/news/news.php?newsid=3142

- Three Receive Rankin Awards at ISU
  http://www.indstate.edu/news/news.php?newsid=3141

- National Council on Family Relations Honors ISU Senior
  http://indstate.edu/news/news.php?newsid=3124

- Two Presented President's Award for Civic and Community
  Leadership
  http://www.indstate.edu/news/news.php?newsid=3093

- Students Awarded for Involvement with Nonprofit
  Leadership Alliance http://www.indianastatesman.com/
  features/students-awarded-for-involvement-with-nonprofit-
  leadership-alliance-1.2774545#.Utkp9dJdW2c

- Student Earns Scholarship from National American
  Humanics Organization
  http://www.indstate.edu/news/news.php?newsid=2322

- Three American Humanics Students Earn Leadership
  Honors
  http://www.indstate.edu/news/news.php?newsid=2209

- NextGen Scholarships Awarded to Two ISU Students
  http://www.indstate.edu/news/news.php?newsid=1886

Intercollegiate Athletic Departments and Teams
College athletics, in most cases, are governed by the NCAA. The
NCAA has rules that are enforced and monitored by its campus
Athletic Compliance Officers. In short, head coaches are only

allowed to require a student-athlete to commit twenty hours per week for "countable athletically related activities," such as competition, coaches meetings, practice, weight training, conditioning, and participation in camps/clinics (IUPUI n.d.). However, the head coach can require hours for fundraising activities, public relations events, promotional activities, community services, and outreach and have it considered "noncountable athletically related activities" (IUPUI n.d., 2). In short, a head coach can require a lot of athletes in the area of community service and it not count toward the twenty hour requirement. If you play your cards right, you can tap into this resource through a college athletic department.

College athletic departments can provide an immense amount of assistance to a local nonprofit organization—if you have the right connections. First and foremost, most head coaches of men's and women's athletic teams encourage and even require community service for their athletes. However, the vast majority of the intercollegiate athletic departments in the United States do not have a community-service coordinator as a central hub for all athletes. It should be mentioned that some athletic departments are partnering with their campus's center for community engagement or center for service-learning to coordinate athletes' community-service hours.

The next thing to understand is that there tends to be no rhyme or reason regarding why or how much a head coach requires community service of his or her athletes. Ultimately, having athletes visible in the community builds brand awareness and goodwill, the expectation being that ticket sales and attendance at games and competition will increase. Each head coach, like any other human, donor, or volunteer, has one or more causes close to his or her heart that he or she has an affinity for. Your job is to get to know the head coaches at the local college campus, build a relationship with them, and get to know what causes they are passionate about.

Then, you might offer them an opportunity to engage their teams in your organization in some way.

For example, at one NCAA Division I institution, the head basketball coach has an affinity for animal welfare, so he has accepted an opportunity to be engaged with the local humane society. In one instance, this head coach served as a public advocate for animal welfare by being in a commercial as a local celebrity for the humane society, free of charge. In another instance, the same basketball coach arranged to have the same humane society featured at a basketball game by allowing the humane society to bring a variety of animals onto the basketball floor at half time to promote the animal adoption program and volunteer opportunities, as well as to have space in the basketball arena concourse before, during, and after the game. This head coach also participated as a local celebrity in a fundraising event for the humane society.

Local Celebrity Waiters Raise Money for a Cause

http://www.mywabashvalley.com/story/d/story/local-celebrity-waiters-raise-money-for-a-cause/15336/8q5KoCMfVkqta-QJE1OZVg

The same head basketball coach partnered with the American Cancer Society for Coaches vs. Cancer.

Lawmakers Wearing Sneakers at the Statehouse

http://www.mywabashvalley.com/story/d/story/lawmakers-wearing-sneakers-at-thestatehouse/39680/-4aDDwD6yUiashlhV_vl8g

The same humane society was able to successfully partner with the same university's baseball team to create a promotional night called Bark at the Park, where fans could bring their dogs to the baseball game.

http://www.gosycamores.com/ViewArticle.dbml?ATCLID=1147526

Another good example is a university's women's golf team that had a student-athlete on scholarship and also on the autism spectrum. For some time the coaches and players did not understand the behavior of the player. Eventually, the team, with the help of the player's family, became educated about autism spectrum disorder and rallied around this player. The team then started participating in local community-service opportunities to promote autism awareness and to raise money for Autism Speaks. As a group, the head coach, assistant coach, and several players even served as the keynote speakers at an Autism Speaks fundraising event.

As the examples above demonstrate, an intercollegiate athletic department can be an excellent resource for the nonprofit organization where you work. There are a couple of other things you should know about collaborating with head coaches and student-athletes.

- Head coaches come and go often, based on wins and losses, so plan to start the relationship-building process over and over again as new head coaches are hired.

- Head coaches are the ones that require community service, but assistant coaches are the ones that tend to track it with each player. Assistant coaches tend to come and go more quickly than head coaches. Be prepared to always be training up the new assistant coach.

- Many athletic directors create an intracollegiate athletic competition between the sports teams on their campuses, often called the Athletic Director's (AD) Cup. Frequently, one of the areas in which points can be gained is community service. Nonprofit leaders need to make it easy for head coaches to encourage their athletes to complete community-service hours at their agencies.

- Just as your nonprofit organization needs support and attendance, so do the athletic teams, so plan on buying season tickets, donating to sports team via the college's foundation, and generally being visible as a fan. Also, promote the sports team that is serving your organization in your office facilities, and find a way to bring your staff, volunteers, and clients to a game at least once a year as a group. Mutual reciprocity in any partnership is expected.

Honors Programs

Honors programs tend to have the best and brightest students who are the most engaged and intrinsically motivated. Done right, on time, and under budget is the type of work you can come to expect from honors students. Most honors programs have affiliated faculty, as well as a registered student organization. Another opportunity for nonprofit organizations to tap into is the undergraduate honors thesis requirement that many colleges expect of their honors students. An honors thesis tends to be at least a semester-long research project conducted by the individual student under the guidance of a professor. Many of the projects listed in chapter 2 can be designed to count for the honors thesis requirement. For example, nonprofit program evaluation projects and stewardship and donor recognition projects have been counted as honors thesis projects at some institutions. Also, graduate-level master's theses and projects can encompass a nonprofit organization project. An example of this is staff and volunteer training on pluralistic leadership and diversity that was produced for HealthCare Excel by a human resources management graduate student.

International Student Affairs/Global Engagement

Many colleges have had international student affairs offices for years, and now those offices are transforming into Centers for Global Engagement on many campuses. These offices do more than assist in bringing international students to their campuses. They also facilitate domestic faculty, staff, and students in becoming engaged globally by going overseas for short-term and long-term study abroad, for sabbatical, international conference travel, and for international alumni relations. The campus investment in technology has also facilitated a variety of global engagement opportunities for students, faculty, staff, and nonprofit community partners while never having to leave your office or hometown. Depending on your organization's mission, if it has an international angle, or even an international component within your organization's strategic goals and objectives, a college's international student affairs office or center for global engagement could provide the right partnership and resources for your organization.

Student Centers, Student Unions, and Indoor and Outdoor Facilities

One of the real tangible resources that a college can provide a nonprofit organization, especially a small nonprofit with little or no facility, office, meeting, or indoor and outdoor special event space, is often free or low-cost facility rental. Often these facilities are managed through the staff at colleges' student centers or student unions.

For example, Indiana State University has hosted the Special Olympics Indiana Summer Games for forty years. This includes housing athletes in residence halls, feeding athletes, staff, and volunteers in residence hall dining, as well as coordinating opening ceremonies at the basketball arena, socials and dances in the student union, and athletic competition throughout the athletic and recreational indoor and outdoor facilities.

Moreover, at Indiana State University, the campus has hosted a variety of other nonprofit organizational events, such as: the Indiana Youth Institute's Youth Worker Cafes (http://www.indstate.edu/news/news.php?newsid=3341); About Special Kids Inc.'s Special Education Workshop (http://www.indstate.edu/news/news.php?newsid=2830) and a Planning for Your Dependent with Special Needs: Making Their Future More Secure Workshop (http://www.bridgesofindiana.com/index.php?option=com_eventlist&view=details&id=228); as well as Summer Camp Staff Recruitment Fairs for the American Camp Association-Indiana Section (http://www.indstate.edu/news/news-pre2008.php?newsid=1522); Cub Scout Pinewood Derbies, galas, and sporting events in ballrooms, gyms, pools, and environmental education facilities.

Although parking can be an issue on college campuses, especially during business hours, the benefits far outweigh the drawbacks when looking for free or low-cost facilities with on-site catering and a cadre of available students to volunteer at your event. For the university, it is good marketing and public relations to bring a variety of constituents to campus. It's also an incentive to nonprofit organizations to serve as community partners with faculty and staff trying to create community engagement and service-learning opportunities within the mission of the university for its students.

To secure space, you will need someone who works on campus, usually a full-time faculty or staff member, to have some connection to your organization as a volunteer or board member. The sponsoring faculty or staff member will typically need to legitimately connect the use of a college facility to a class assignment or service initiative that clearly ties to his or her role at the university. Also, you will want to establish relationships with relevant registered student organizations. They can host your event as a part of their allotment of free rentals per semester on most campuses—as long as the facility use is ethically and genuinely connected to that RSO's mission and work.

Technology and Telecommunications Assistance

Colleges can also provide nonprofit organizations with a number of technology and telecommunication services. For example, DePauw University runs an amazing program called Computer Technology

Enhancement Program (CTEP) (http://www.depauw.edu/offices/ctep/). CTEP is a student-led, faculty supervised program that distributes refurbished computers to qualifying organizations and individuals in need. Its goal is to bridge the digital divide in rural west-central Indiana. CTEP also provides community workshops and Internet resources. "CTEP collects computers (towers and laptops) and parts from DePauw University, local schools, and the surrounding community. CTEP staff members test the equipment and clear old information from computers. CTEP prepares computers with Microsoft Windows 7 and installs a range of free software and programs for a new user" (http://www.depauw.edu/offices/ctep/).

Another good example of technology services that a nonprofit organization can access from a college is website design, hosting, and maintenance services. Indiana State University provides a service called Sycamore Technology Solutions (STS). "Sycamore Technology Solutions is a student-managed and operated company designed to fulfill the technology goals and support needs of the United Way member agencies and other not-for-profit organizations. STS was created to give junior and senior students majoring in computer science, electronics and computer science, information technology, management information systems or other computer-related majors a chance to get some real-world experience in their fields" (http://www.compact.org/program-models/program-models-technology-andor-science-in-service-programs/sycamore-technology-solutions/1646/). For more information, please visit http://stsweb.indstate.edu/~sts/

Given the right connection to the right faculty or staff member, colleges can also meet the technology needs of nonprofit organization by creating and hosting web forms for internal reporting, such as a ScoutReach Online Incident and Accident Reporting System (https://indstate.qualtrics.com/SE/?SID=SV_6hF3WeAGIIW6sPG) or a ScoutReach Program Evaluation Online Site Visit Observation Form https://indstate.qualtrics.com/SE/?SID=SV_ abYsdUrCE0uUB9i).

Also, data analysis services can be accessed for community needs assessment, program evaluation, or any other data analysis need, by contacting a variety of academic disciplines listed above. However, educational psychology is always a good place to start for statistical needs and consulting.

Finally, given the right connection to the right faculty or staff member, colleges can host conference calls for nonprofit organizations, with the conference bridge calling technology. As always, finding the right faculty or staff member means engaging that person in your organization in a volunteer, advisory, board member, membership, or consulting role that ties to his or her discipline, teaching, research, and/or service roles, so that the faculty or staff member can ethically use college resources for his or her work with your organization.

Surplus Auctions

To bridge from the section above on technology and telecommunications assistance, colleges also have surplus equipment that goes to auction on a regular basis. This includes desktop and laptop computers, as well as a variety of other technology hardware that a nonprofit organization might need. Surplus auctions can also include office equipment, furniture, desks, filing cabinets, chairs, chalkboards, etc.—all things that nonprofit organizations may need, and for a rock-bottom price. Typically, to learn about surplus auctions at a campus near you, you would go to the college's website and search for the Facilities or Purchasing and Central Receiving Department.

Interprofessional Education (IPE) Teams

A major benefit nonprofit organizations can glean from academic partnerships is access to a wide variety of expertise, as students from different majors and disciplines can come together to help identify and meet the needs of community organizations. Several such partnerships have emerged at Indiana State University, particularly as that institution includes interprofessional education in the strategic plan of its College of Nursing, Health, and Human Services. For example, students from such disciplines as nursing, public health, dietetics, and health administration work together to educate the campus and community about various health behaviors at the annual Wellness Bash.

Another good example of a NPO reaping great benefit from a college, while students gain critical learning experience at the organization, is through a health promotion and aging course. This class works specifically with a nearby grassroots organization called Senior Education Ministries (SEM), where they collect data from participants in a health education program. Students, in conjunction with older adults participating in the NPO's programs, identify key health behaviors, procedures, and issues that are of concern to older adults, such as information on knee replacement surgery and rehabilitation. Relying on their diverse educational backgrounds and career aspirations, students then develop information sheets to convey useful and relevant information to older adult participants in SEM programs. The interprofessional nature of this activity provides a rich and more meaningful product that meets the needs of participants in the NPO's programs. Furthermore, the limited time of the small staff of SEM prevents the NPO from creating such useful information sheets by themselves. In the end, students benefit from actively participating in research and the creation of educational materials by relying on and applying the knowledge and skills gained through their discipline-based coursework, while a local organization benefits from acquiring high-quality materials that enable them to better accomplish their mission and objectives.

Office of Communication and Marketing

Almost every college campus has a communications, marketing, community, and public relations office. The secret here is do everything you can to make friends with the folks in these offices. They are tasked with promoting the good, student-centered work that is happening on their campuses in order to increase student recruitment and retention. These offices are also tasked with branding their campuses and controlling the message and reputation of the institutions. Most colleges will welcome the opportunity to market college and community collaborations that highlight their faculty, staff, and students, as well as your organization. Colleges are now quite adept at social media marketing, too, which is a quick and free resource for your organization.

To make friends with these folks, always say please and thank you—multiple times. Always give as much lead time as possible so as to not put undue stress and time demands on the staff. Be willing to work and to coteach their student staff assistants, as well as to be patient. Do everything you can to make it as easy as possible for the college to promote your organization.

Having bona fide college-sponsored media links on the Internet can be used in a variety of ways, particularly by including such news stories and online video segments in future grant applications to secure funding for your organization. Colleges have the hardware and software to produce typically expensive marketing materials for your organization, as long as you're willing to share credit with the college, faculty, staff, and students.

College communication and marketing offices are always looking for ways to promote their campuses. Anytime faculty, staff, and students receive external awards from local organizations, or state or national professional associations, it gives the office something to highlight. The message here is simple: recognize your college partners with awards from your organization and nominate them for awards from the community (e.g., from the United Way,

Chamber of Commerce, etc.), as well as nominating them for state and national awards from relevant professional organizations. Take care of your campus movers and shakers and they will take care of you!

Distance Education, Continued Education, and E-Service-Learning

Don't forget the opportunities that exist by having distance-education students serve your organization from afar through the power of e-mail, Skype, and so on (Schaumleffel 2014b). Two major trends in higher education are (1) significant increases in community engagement and service-learning and (2) significant increases in online distance-education courses. These two trends are beginning to collide, and professors are looking to use the educational effectiveness of community engagement in distance education by using the power of the Internet to close the geographic divide. Waldner, McGorry, and Widener (2012, 125) define e-service-learning in this way: "when the instructional component, the service component, or both are conducted online."

An example of e-service-learning is having distance-education students develop nonprofit program evaluation logic models and grant proposals for a nonprofit organization that is close to their geographic location. In this case one student will work with one organization face-to-face.

Waldner, McGorry, and Widener (2010, 839) acknowledged an even newer trend in higher education called extreme e-service-learning (XE-SL) and define it as "service learning where both the instruction and the service occur 100% percent online." For example, one distance-education professor, who teaches nonprofit management and fundraising, is having distance-education graduate students partner with one nonprofit organization as a group to develop the NPO's annual fund direct-mail letter. All students in the course will collaborate under the professor's guidance using wiki technology via the college's online learning management system to coproduce the annual fund letter for the same organization. To lean more about this project, read:

Community Engagement Goes Cyber: New Nonprofit Classes at Indiana State

http://indstate.edu/news/news.php?newsid=4133

Waldner, McGorry, and Widener (2012, 123–124) stated,

"online learning is a facilitator rather than a barrier to service-learning. E-service-learning holds the potential to transform both service-learning and online learning by freeing service-learning from geographical constraints, and by equipping online learning with a tool to promote engagement. Thus, e-service-learning is not a mere pedagogical curiosity; rather, it is a key to the future of service-learning."

"E-service-learning is an ideal marriage of sorts because it overcomes limitations of both service-learning and online learning. E-service-learning frees service-learning from place-based access or geographical constraints. E-service-learning also overcomes what some consider a key limitation to online learning—a perceived lack of interaction" (Waldner, McGorry, & Widener. 2012, 126).

Beyond the for-credit distance-education course opportunities discussed above, nonprofit leaders should also seek out noncredit and community-based continued education seminars and workshops. Many campuses administratively house both for-credit and noncredit courses within the same department, division, or college. It is not uncommon for colleges to offer a variety of free or low-cost seminars and workshops that take place on-campus, in the community, and even online, related to nonprofit administration (e.g., fundraising, grant proposal preparation, logic modeling, program evaluation) and youth work (e.g., mentoring, juvenile crime, behavior management).

Faculty and Staff and Community-Service Leave Policy
College faculty and staff make excellent volunteers, as well as board and advisory committee members. For example, the director of annual giving at the local college's foundation or office of institutional advancement can make an excellent fundraising chairperson, signature event coordinator, or even help your agency establish and implement a donor management system, direct-mail campaign, direct e-mail campaign, online and social media fundraising, as well as a phone solicitation campaign or a gift acceptance policy. Another good example is campus custodial, facilities, maintenance, and travel pool foremen and superintendents can make excellent facilities advisory committee chairpersons.

Some campuses have even implemented a community-service leave policy. A community-service leave policy, although it differs from campus to campus, basically allows a full-time, benefits-eligible employee to take time away from work at the college during typically scheduled work hours to serve your organization as a volunteer. Employees are typically allowed to participate in community-service leave for organizations for about fifteen hours per academic year, but please note that it varies tremendously from campus to campus, depending on the reason for community-service leave. Some service opportunities are allotted more hours away from campus, such as disaster and emergency volunteer service.

Oftentimes full-time tenured and tenure-track professors do not get community-service leave, since service is part of the normal expectation of the job, along with teaching, research, advising, etc. In this case, it is critical that the faculty member gets what he or she needs from a partnership with your organization for his or her annual performance review. You should have open and frank discussion with potential partners about what they need out of a partnership.

Campus Networking

As you can see, colleges have an amazing amount of time, treasure, and talent on campus that can be channeled to your organization if you and your organization have the right relationships across campus. Finding ways to have a continual, sustainable presence on campus and finding the right go-to person, or people, on your local campus is the key to generating resources for your organization. For more on getting started with finding the right faculty partner, keep reading through to chapter 5!

References

Bloom, B. S., ed. *Taxonomy of Educational Objectives: The Classification of Educational Goals, handbook I, cognitive domain.* (New York: Longmans, Green, 1956).

Indiana University-Purdue University Indianapolis (IUPUI). (n.d.). *Countable Athletically Related Activities.* Retrieved May 6, 2014, from http://www.iupui.edu/~jagsncaa/_Assets/docs/rules_ed/CARA.pdf

Schaumleffel, N. A. *Nonprofit Leadership Like it Oughta Be: Normative Perpetual Mission-Focused Experience Management Cycle.* Presentation conducted synchronously online via the High Impact Webinar Series of the Nonprofit Leadership Alliance, Kansas City, MO. (2014a, February).

Schaumleffel, N. A. *Assessing Community Engagement and Service-Learning Outcomes in the Online Environment: A Case Study from Fundraising Education.* Presentation conducted at the Assessment Institute in Indianapolis, Indianapolis, IN. (2014b, October)

US Department of Education, Federal Student Aid. (n.d.). *2013–2014 Federal Student Aid Handbook, vol. 6*: 6–80. Retrieved May 6, 2014, from http://ifap.ed.gov/fsahandbook/attachments/1314FSAHbk Vol6Ch2.pdf

Waldner, L. S.; S. Y. McGorry; M. C. Widener. "E-service Learning: The Evolution of Service-Learning to Engage a Growing Online Student Population." *Journal of Higher Education Outreach and Engagement 16* (2) (2012): 123–150. Retrieved from http://open-journals.libs.uga.edu/index.php/jheoe/article/view/792

Resources

Leading the Way: Autism-friendly Youth Organization Guide. (New York: Autism Speaks, 2013). Retrieved from http://www.autismspeaks. org/family-services/youth-organizations

Indiana Nonprofit Resource Network
http://www.inrn.org/

Indiana University-Purdue University Indianapolis: Countable Athletically Related Activities http://www.iupui.edu/~jagsncaa/_ Assets/docs/rules_ed/CARA.pdf

Indiana Youth Institute Consulting Services
http://www.iyi.org/consulting-services.aspx

Indiana Youth Institute Kids Count Data Book
http://www.iyi.org/reports.aspx

US Department of Education, Federal Student Aid. *2013–2014 Federal Student Aid Handbook, vol. 6.* (see chapter 2, The Federal Work-Study Program).
http://ifap.ed.gov/fsahandbook/attachments/1314FSAHb kVol6Ch2.pdf

CHAPTER 4:

Why Would Students and Faculty Work Free of Charge (or Below Market Value) for Nonprofit Organizations?

Nathan A. Schaumleffel, PhD, Indiana State University

Tina M. Kruger, PhD, Indiana State University

Marilyn Lake McElwain, MFA, University of Indianapolis

The Community Technology Enrichment Program (CTEP) is a DePauw University-affiliated organization that addresses the digital divide issue. CTEP accepts used yet viable computers from area businesses, refurbishes them, and then distributes the systems to qualifying organizations and individuals; CTEP also conducts workshops on technology for local residents. CTEP operates on a shoestring budget with only two or three students receiving work-study funds; the majority of students participate either as part of a service-learning course, as a way to gain valuable real-world experience, or simply from a desire to apply their skills and interests to a program that benefits the community.
—Dr. Douglas E. Harms, Community Technology
Enrichment Program

As mentioned in chapter 3, collaboration between nonprofit organizations and colleges can and should be mutually beneficial, like the CTEP program at DePauw University. Mutually beneficial partnerships will meet the needs of all individuals and organizations in the partnership. In the case of college and community partnerships, the partnerships will meet the needs of: the organization; the organization's clients, staff, and volunteers; the college; the students; and the faculty member.

As a nonprofit professional, board member, or volunteer, you may still be asking yourself, so what's in it for the college? All of this free and low-cost stuff in chapter 3 seems too good to be true. This chapter presents the truth of the matter.

Just as a nonprofit organization has a mission statement, strategic plan, goals, and objectives—all chock-full of needs and expenses—so do colleges. Often embedded in those strategic plans are goals related to student achievement, student retention, and student graduation rates. Campus discussions regarding how to achieve college goals for student achievement inevitably include the following: objectives related to instructor teaching performance evaluation; academic advisement evaluations; and student-learning assessment at the degree, program, course, and even lesson or module level. Student-learning assessment is a very similar process to nonprofit program evaluation, such as the evaluation process implemented by the United Way in recent years, where organizations must document with data that the programs funded by the United Way are making a measurable difference in achieving the human development goals of the NPO.

In this chapter, a brief overview of student-learning assessment will be given, and then a discussion of benefits of community engagement for students and faculty will follow. The nonprofit executive director, board member, or volunteer reading this book should leave this chapter knowing that your organization is an important part of the educational experience for students, and that your organization is an equally vital part of a college-community partnership. You are essentially a community coprofessor and the faculty you work with should see you this way, too. Colleges need your organization just as much as your organization needs the time, treasure, and talent available from the college. Your organization can provide the valuable, real-world, hands-on experiential learning opportunities that students desire through a community engagement partnership. These learning opportunities are simply not possible without partnerships with NPOs. Well-designed and managed community engagement partnerships may increase the chance for students to achieve the learning outcomes of their course and may increase teaching evaluation scores of a professor by his or her students and colleagues. These potential benefits are worth the investment of college resources in your organization.

Student-learning Assessment
Traditionally, colleges have educated and assessed students' competence on-campus in the classroom via lectures, chalkboards, whiteboards, Power Point, quizzes, exams, fictitious projects about the real world, and term papers. Over the years, faculty have worked to redesign classes to enhance student learning by using active learning strategies that motivate students to learn at higher levels of Bloom's (1956) taxonomy. Faculty want students to learn more than the fundamental knowledge and facts of their courses and then regurgitate those facts on a final exam. Faculty want students to develop as leaders, decision makers, problem solvers, critical thinkers, goal setters, visionaries, and self-motivated professionals and citizens. Faculty want students to be able to apply information, analyze and synthesize different perspectives, and have the ability to evaluate policies and organizational decisions. Opportunities for students to learn through application, synthesis, and evaluation are significantly enhanced through community-based learning projects with organizations like yours!

To achieve higher levels of student learning, many faculty are actively seeking out and coproducing community engagement projects through partnerships with nonprofit organizations. Faculty members who are heavily engaged in these sorts of projects are called engaged scholars. In these partnerships, resources flow from the college to the nonprofit organization, and learning opportunities flow from the nonprofit organization to the student. These community engagement opportunities with colleges are fantastic teaching and learning laboratories for students and, like a lottery for nonprofit human and financial resource needs, you can't win if you don't play!

A key issue for both faculty teaching classes and NPOs accomplishing their missions is assessment. The goal of assessment is to determine how well the person or program being assessed does what he, she or it are supposed to do. Teachers use assessment to see what their students can do in terms of the course objectives (Astin and Antonio 2012), and NPOs use assessment to understand the organization's strengths and weaknesses (Center for Nonprofit Excellence n.d.). The nonprofit sector uses the term program evaluation for the process of a NPO assessing the effectiveness of its programs and services achieving predetermined goals and objectives (Schaumleffel 2014).

When colleges partner with NPOs in community engagement projects, both groups have vested interests in assessing the outcomes of the interaction. In short, mutually beneficial college-community partnerships need to measurably improve the effectiveness of a nonprofit program or service and increase student learning. Teachers need to understand the extent to which the project contributed to an improvement in the students' ability to demonstrate, discuss, summarize, construct (and a host of other verbs based on Bloom's taxonomy) material related to the course. NPOs need to understand the extent to which the organization is accomplishing its mission and how the community engagement project helped in the accomplishment of the mission. These two assessment processes don't need to be entirely separate efforts.

When NPOs work as coeducators with college teachers, and both partners work together on the community engagement project and the assessment activities, all collaborators can walk away with the information they need to do their jobs well. For example, in a community engagement project with an NPO dedicated to promoting health and well-being among older adults, students in a health promotion and aging course conducted focus groups with participants in programs run by the NPO. The focus groups concentrated on discussion of what participants liked and disliked about the programs, what they would like to see in future iterations of the programs, and what suggestions they had for improving the programs. The students used the information to guide their projects in the course, including researching the topics of interest to the older adults and developing information sheets on those topics (e.g., knee replacement surgery, cardiac bypass surgery, diabetes maintenance).

To assess student learning, the students were asked to write a reflection paper on their experience in the focus groups and to identify what older adult participants said they liked about the program and what they would like to see in future programs. This course-based assessment generated useful data for the NPO partner as they were able to use the information provided by the students to determine how well they were accomplishing their mission. Thus, both partners derived useful information from the assessment process, enabling all partners to perform their needed tasks better.

Students Needs and Benefits from Community Engagement

Opportunities for college-community partnerships primarily arise from two sources, either the community organization determines a specific need that requires additional resources, or the college desires a community partnership to meet the objectives set forth by the curriculum of a particular field of study, a goal of the college's strategic plan, or purely for good PR. In many cases, the mission of the college may focus on community partnerships that have a long-standing history of mutual benefit or reciprocity. While the college provides necessary resources, students receive the bene-fits of learning through service engagement in community-based organizations.

Much research has been conducted over the last twenty years on the benefits of community engagement and service-learning. In 2008, Dan Simonet from Minnesota Campus Compact compiled literature on the vast student-development benefits of service-learning. In short, community engagement projects are wonder-ful opportunities to achieve student learning outcomes. For a full report of the student benefits of service-learning, please review Simonet's (2008) work at

http://www.compact.org/wp-content/uploads/resources/downloads/MN-SL_and_academic_success.pdf

Community engagement is a viable instructional approach with important benefits to students. In addition to the application of course content, students are given opportunities for personal growth as they experience and gain insight into the diverse issues that challenge members of a community and the needs of agencies whose mission it is to assist those individuals.

In terms of one class of students, students may be enrolled in the same course from many different majors, such as allied health sciences, sociology, psychology, sport management, education, and visual and performing arts. Students apply critical thinking skills in the classroom both prior to and during the service component. They see real-life situations and consequences of decisions that af-fect both the community partner and the participants, "integrat-ing service with self," while better comprehending the relevancy of material. Jones and Hill asserted "how a student understands, constructs and engages in community service is influenced by the socially constructed identities they bring to the experience" (2003, 533).

The enthusiasm and excitement experienced by students when working with a community partner and participants makes that experience even more relevant. Realizing that they have contributed in some way to the betterment of others is a primary outcome of community engagement. Students come to understand their own strengths and self-efficacy, often drawing on skills that they did not previously know they possessed, or in many cases they will begin to acquire new skills to meet new challenges. These skills may be in the areas of communication, collaborative teamwork, problem solving, organization, planning, and coordination. They must be flexible enough to adapt to new responsibilities and to take on new roles. Because students may be involved in needs assessment, research and other activities related to the projects, it's hoped they will develop expertise in areas that help prepare them for graduate school or professional fields. They will develop a sense of place in society and a commitment to being a strong citizen of the world. Once students gain a better understanding of community issues, many are motivated to act in ways that bring about change and social justice. They will learn new behaviors and develop attitudes that are the result of enhanced civic engagement. Students are challenged to enhance knowledge of economic, political, and cultural understanding in both local and international settings.

For many students, personal growth is often the most noted outcome or benefit of community engagement. Because students reflect extensively on the impact that helping others has had on them personally, they come to know the immersion experience as a character-building vehicle that helps them become more well rounded, while creating a network of contacts and allowing the individual student to better understand diverse populations in communities. For many this revelation of need, mission, or purpose is life-altering in a positive manner. This transformative experience moves the student to become a civically engaged adult, someone who will address the needs of communities in the future.

A good example of the transformative power of community engagement projects is an instance of students at the University of

Indianapolis enrolling in a Spring Term Service Trip to Athens, Greece. Students were challenged in many ways when working with refugees from the Middle East and Africa. Besides learning to communicate with people who spoke little or no English, students were forced to adapt to situations where they used rudimentary skills of drawing and mimicry. Many cultural differences became palpable. Sensitivity and flexibility to work with the refugees was necessary. The English classes grew daily, as both the refugees and service-learning students formulated a process of communication as well as mutual respect. Friendships were developed. Students learned that they had previously untapped abilities. They also learned about working with a refugee-relief agency, which provided food, clothing, and language lessons in Greek and English.

Students may also benefit by counting service hours to a NPO not only for course-based experiences but also for service hours for sororities, fraternities, and athletics. Students may even continue their relationships with your organization by partnering to complete their honors, senior, or master's thesis or capstone project. Students may also list their service-learning experiences with your organization on their resume, cocurricular records, and in their professional portfolios or e-portfolios. During these projects, students sometimes connect with the agency, staff, and clients to the point where they continue to volunteer after the project is over. They may serve as an intern, hire in as part-time staff (e.g., Federal Work-Study or AmeriCorps employment), or even hire into a full-time staff position. The early career exposure to professional networking opportunities through community engagement projects is invaluable to students, as they gain community mentors as well as professional references. There is a parallel benefit to the community organization in serving as a regular community engagement partner. The organization effectively gets the pick of the litter, so to speak, and projects serve as on-site interviews for staff positions that could be filled by local students.

Faculty Needs and Benefits from Community Engagement

Managing Risk

Most people in colleges and nonprofit organizations want to help youth, people, families, and communities. They want to make a positive difference and make a measurable impact! People also, for the most part, would like to keep their jobs so that they can support themselves and their dependents. It's that simple. You want to keep your job. Students want to get a job. Faculty members want to keep their jobs, as well as move up and earn promotion, tenure, and perhaps administrative posts. Recognizing this basic fact will make you a better partner to faculty members. Taking the time to generally understand the faculty evaluation system, even though it differs tremendously between colleges, departments, and disciplines, is critical for you to be the best possible partner—the one who gets the most time, treasure, and talent from a faculty member.

If you decide to engage with colleges for community engagement projects, you need to understand the balance that tenured and tenure-track faculty members must maintain when agreeing to provide your organization with technical expertise, human resources, and financial capital. Most faculty are required to be successful in three broad areas of work: teaching, scholarship, and service. These three areas of work often compete for the faculty member's time and often make him or her feel like three dogs tied at the tails and running in three different directions. If faculty are to be successful in retention, tenure, promotion, and posttenure reviews, they have to work smart by aligning their responsibilities so that one area benefits the other. Unlike high school teachers, college professors are not just teachers, as teaching represents only a percentage of their responsibilities, often in the 30–40 percent range for regional state universities and as little as 5–10 percent for large flagship research-intensive universities.

As a nonprofit representative, when learning about the three traditional roles of faculty (i.e., teaching, research, and service), you must comprehensively understand what the service requirement is. By doing so you can better situate your needs within the faculty member's workload, as well as conceptually see the connection between the faculty member's service to your organization and his or her teaching responsibilities and scholarly agenda.

Service as the Center of Teaching and Scholarship:
Three Birds with One Stone

Now, let's further explore the faculty service requirement. Although service is required, it is not just community service to local nonprofit organizations. The faculty service requirement also includes internal service at the department, college, and university levels, as well as external service to professional associations, government, and local nonprofit organizations. At some institutions, international service is also becoming important.

The service requirement is one that can take a largely disproportionate amount of the faculty member's time with little return on investment during the personnel evaluation cycle. In short, at many colleges, although service is required, it often counts for 5 percent or less of the faculty member's annual evaluation. That 5 percent is for all service, not just service to nonprofit organizations, which makes it critical for the faculty member to be very selective in managing his or her time and commitments to all areas of service. Faculty can more than meet the evaluation service requirement without embarking on service to nonprofit organizations, much less embarking on complicated community-based service-learning class projects.

So, with teaching responsibilities at 40 percent of a faculty member's workload, and service at as much as 10 percent of that workload, a faculty member must still carve out time to produce scholarly work, which equals 50 percent of the annual evaluation.

All of this must be managed while university administrators, students, and nonprofit partners continually ask more from them. What Schaumleffel, Malaby, and Frank found is that when a nonprofit executive, board member, or volunteer requests assistance from a professor, the nonprofit representative "must realize that community engagement and service-learning is risky business for pretenure faculty and that faculty must manage risk when making decisions to conduct pro bono consulting or to orchestrate complicated community-based class projects." (2010, 32).

"Community service and engagement is growing in importance on campuses because its ideals connect closely with modern university mission statements" (Schaumleffel et al. 2010, 32). Yet, "in Indiana such engagement often is not meaningfully recognized in terms of tenure and promotion...." (Schaumleffel et al. 2010, 33). "What is happening in Indiana is reflected nationwide, as noted by O'Meara (1997), who conducted a study examining approximately 400 tenure and promotion documents and found that only 6.5 percent of the sample universities had changed their policies to better encourage and reward faculty service" (Schaumleffel et al. 2010, 33).

However, the good news is that in recent years, community engagement has become recognized as a viable vehicle through which the three faculty roles of teaching, scholarship, and service can be integrated succinctly, if the faculty member can conduct the academic concert, so to speak (Frank, Malaby, Bates, Coulter-Kern, Fraser-Burgess, Jamison, Stalker-Prokopy, & Schaumleffel. 2011; Schaumleffel et al. 2010).

Improving Teaching Through Service

"Typically, university to community assistance has been looked upon as a two-way partnership that ensures benefit to the agency in the form of free service and to the students as a quality real-world learning experience" (Schaumleffel et al. 2010, 32). Throughout chapters 3 and 4, we have clearly documented the benefits of community engagement projects for the students and the nonprofit organizations, as well as the risk to faculty. Now, we would like to discuss the benefits of community engagement projects for the faculty member.

Kezar and Rhodes (2001) assert that service-learning connects to all three areas of faculty responsibility: teaching, research, and scholarship. In a truly reciprocal arrangement, mutual respect is key. For faculty members, any service engagement partnership should address three distinct needs in the following priority order: (1) the student-learning objectives/outcomes; (2) the mission, goals, and objectives of the partnering organization; and (3) the faculty member's professional-development needs (Frank et al. 2011; Schaumleffel et al. 2010).

Faculty should work closely with the community partner to respond to community needs, responding with their own abilities and training. It is inappropriate for faculty to develop a project for their own interests without meeting a need that has been specified by the community partner. While faculty wants to provide service, which is also desired by the institution, the service project must be acceptable and needed by the partner

Building a college-community partnership that is based on this three-way benefit will motivate faculty to actively engage in the partnership, causing an immersion experience that forges new community relationships. This benefits students, organizations, their clients, and their educational institutions. In short, if the projects are planned and implemented with the understanding that the faculty member is equally deserving of professional benefit from the partnership, then the faculty member will channel time, treasure, and talent to your organization.

When looking at college-community partnerships as a three-way relationship, projects can develop that bring benefits beyond the initial collaboration. They can drive future interactions that are more extensive in mission-focus, influence, and long-term, sustainable consequence, such as community development outcomes. Faculty, students, and community partners can have an impact on bringing about change in the community itself. Impact studies, neighborhood surveys, needs assessments, program evaluations, and other projects that help generate research for community development may begin with collaboration between faculty and community partners.

However, when faculty spend time on service, especially service to a nonprofit organization, the service must do the following: improve student and peer teaching evaluation ratings; generate positive public relations on and off campus; possibly lead to teaching and service awards from the college, the nonprofit organization, the local community, or a state or national professional association; as well as create opportunities for scholarly work.

As previously mentioned, faculty must manage risk by generating higher student and peer teaching evaluation ratings, as well as receive teaching awards for their community-based learning efforts. These teaching goals can be achieved by faculty successfully implementing community engagement and service-learning experiences in their courses as alternative methods of exploring and applying course content.

Faculty mature and develop through the course revitalization process and through community engagement partnerships. After substantial sharing and assessment take place, they become more in-tune with community needs and assets. This process tends to sharpen the professional practice skills of faculty while improving learning opportunities for students, since community engagement and service-learning often are focused on developing strategies and solutions to community problems. The problem-based learning strategy that many community engagement projects take their shape from can be an exciting approach to teaching. It requires community-based research, as well as review of literature to develop the most sound and best practices for addressing community needs.

Like students, faculty learn from the nonprofit partner organizations, as power is balanced with reciprocal sharing of time, information, and resources. These reciprocal relationships are a major benefit to faculty. Like a bottle of fine wine, as faculty mature, they reevaluate and modify courses so that student engagement activities relate to content more effectively, as well as promote a seamless view of learning because educators must link classroom learning with out-of-class experiences. Engaged scholars are constantly gathering up to date information, which becomes part of the annual teaching evaluation process for faculty. They are required to document how they stay current with trends, issues, and problems in their field, and in teaching and learning strategies. Engaged scholars are truly practitioner-professors who not only teach and research but also practice, consult, train, and author! They are full-time academics and full-time practitioners, which is why they are busy, busy, busy people. In short, they simply do not pontificate from the ivory tower, but they engage, practice, reflect, and teach! Besides using faculty service to improve teaching to students and providing free or low-cost consulting for nonprofit organizations, service must also generate scholarly products for faculty.

Producing Scholarship Through Service

College professors not only teach students and provide service, but they also have substantial responsibilities to produce scholarship. Oftentimes...no, most of the time, professors get so busy with prepping for class, teaching, grading, being available for office hours, responding to student e-mails, advising, dealing with academic integrity issues, dealing with helicopter parents (yes, we deal with parents just like middle school and high school teachers, and, of course, nothing is ever their child's fault!), as well as going to faculty governance committee meetings, revising curricula, dealing with personnel committee decisions, collecting and analyzing assessment data, writing grant proposals, and recruiting students that we rarely have time to focus on our scholarship responsibilities.

The basic fact of the matter is that we cannot protect enough time for our scholarship responsibilities. Many professors at regional state universities have 30–40 percent scholarship responsibilities, and at large research-intensive institutions faculty have 60–95 percent scholarship responsibilities. Now, guess what happens when 30–40 percent of your job doesn't get done during the work week because you are too busy teaching and serving your campus, community, and professional associations? You guessed it: engaged scholars work fifty to seventy-five hours per week, including nights, weekends, and holidays, and are only paid for forty of those hours to meet their scholarship responsibilities. If not, they fail, get reprimanded, and may lose their jobs, especially if they are pretenure. An alternative is working more efficiently by improving teaching effectiveness and producing scholarly products from their service.

In light of these time management issues, faculty must manage risk by generating scholarship from their community engagement and service-learning projects. To put things into perspective for those outside the world of college faculty and administration, let's take a look at what senior administrators and senior faculty who make promotion and tenure decisions are saying to early career professors regarding the wise use of their time.

A group of engaged scholars, Frank et al. (2011), asked academic administrators and faculty what steps pretenure faculty could take in documenting service-learning projects to maximize impact for promotion and tenure. The quite negative responses situated service-learning by itself as minimally important to the promotion and tenure process. One respondent noted the following:

They [junior faculty] should make sure it doesn't interfere with their discipline-based, peer-reviewed scholarship. I have nothing against service-learning, but it is a part of teaching methodology and nothing more.

"In fact, a majority of the administrators who responded advised pretenure faculty against engaging in service-learning altogether, noting that doing so could damage their chances for tenure. Even those who noted the value of service-learning in this section of the survey were quick to warn of its dangers for nontenured faculty in the current system" (Schaumleffel et al. 2010, 32).

"Respondents were also unified regarding how service-learning is likely to be counted in promotion and tenure with and without accompanying products. Several respondents answered with the single word 'None' or phrases like 'not a primary criterion' when asked about the value of service-learning (on its own) in the promotion and tenure process. However, when respondents were asked if it is acceptable for 'products' from service-learning (such as peer-reviewed journal articles and conference presentations) to count toward promotion and tenure in the area of scholarship over 70 percent of participants agreed. When considered separately from publications, service-learning was perceived as disproportionally time-consuming relative to its benefits in the promotion and tenure process" (Schaumleffel et al. 2010, 32).

Basically, professors are being told to provide service, but just a little bit, and to not let it get in the way of their scholarship. The bottom line to all of this is that the faculty member who can deliver on partnerships that benefit your organization will not be willing to partner with you if you are not willing to meet his or her needs as well as the students' and your organization's needs (Frank et al. 2011; Schaumleffel et al. 2010). Get your backscratcher out and sharpen it. If you don't, "then it is fair to say that faculty will likely manage their risk and not partner to assist unwilling agencies and professionals" (Schaumleffel et al. 2010, 33). "To be successful in the academic setting, faculty must be selective about the community agencies and professionals with whom they partner, so that the time they spend serving the community generates the necessary 'product' to achieve promotion and tenure" (Schaumleffel et al. 2010, 33). Faculty that turn their service into scholarship and simultaneously enhance their teaching effectiveness are called engaged scholars. They often base their professorship around Boyer's (1990) Model of Scholarship that includes the scholarship of application/engagement and the scholarship of teaching and learning.

Faculty must produce scholarly work and community engagement provides scholarship opportunities for faculty. Scholarly and creative work can take many forms, especially depending on the discipline, but those most recognized by administrators and faculty who make promotion and tenure decisions—and who do not necessarily understand and/or respect engaged scholarship—are the following: peer-reviewed research journal articles; professional magazine articles; presentations at local, regional, state, national, and international scholarly conferences; and funded grant proposals. While qualitative and quantitative research may be required in some departments, other faculty scholarship may take other forms, such as visual art exhibitions, theatrical productions, and photographic or video documentation.

This is the old mantra of publish or perish. And, yes, this attitude still firmly exists even at the four-year colleges that have a tenure system and claim to be teaching institutions. Believe it or not, those required trips to give presentations at state, national, and international conferences are often unfunded, so the expense comes out of the faculty member's pocket. Yep...you heard that right. Professors often have to pay to do their job (at $800–$1,500 per conference trip, on average).

Often faculty complete their scholarship requirements during the summers, when they are not being paid, because they are so busy meeting teaching and service requirements during the nine-month academic year. Also, most people, outside the college world do not realize that most professor contracts are nine-month contracts. So, in effect, faculty are unemployed during the summer but are working to complete the 30–40 percent of their job dedicated to scholarship that they did not have time for during the school year.

Also, you need to understand that most professors who can help the nonprofit organization that provides youth, human, and social services are professors from the social sciences—meaning psychology, sociology, recreation management, nonprofit leadership, social work, human development and family studies, gerontology, etc. Social science professor is a code word on campus for much lower paid than a business professor. Often, business professors (and other fields like physical therapy) are paid $20,000–$30,000 more than a professor in the social sciences. All things being equal—a PhD, first year on the job, same experience level, same teaching load, same scholarly and service expectations, everything the same—they make $20,000-plus more on day one. It's not fair, but it's the truth. Tenure-track social science professors are also typically in their late twenties or early thirties, starting a family, maybe buying their first house, strapped with four to eight years of graduate-education student loan debt, and paying to do their jobs. So, you need to consider what these folks' needs are.

We do not share this insider information with you hoping you will feel sorry for us, or to impress you. But, let's be honest, the media tends to portray professorships as a very cushy job where we come in and teach once or twice a day and go home, and then take three months off each summer while being paid. Contrary to popular belief, summer is not a verb to most professors.

So, what does this mean for a nonprofit partner? How do you use this information to help the faculty partner meet scholarship requirements while he or she is taking valuable time to serve your organization? How can you structure a partnership with a college to make service a professional benefit to the faculty member that will motivate him or her to channel time, treasure, and talent to your organization? The following are some very clear and intentional things you can do.

First, the faculty member, when negotiating a partnership and establishing a project with a nonprofit organization, should share his or her career needs, especially those related to scholarly production. However, most professors will not do this, because it could be perceived as selfish. Just because the faculty member doesn't bring this issue up, doesn't mean you should ignore it. Nonprofit executives, board members, and volunteers should deliberately ask the faculty member this question: What do you need from this partnership for your annual evaluations and long-term career, and, specifically, how can we help you publish something from this project? Then, both parties should ensure that the faculty member's needs also get written into the memorandum of understanding. If you do this for your faculty partner, he or she will turn on the faucet of time, treasure, and talent.

For the faculty member to successfully integrate the scholarship of application/engagement as well as the scholarship of teaching and learning into service projects with your organization, your organization should be willing to allow the professor to collect data, and publish and present the results on a variety of issues based on his or her discipline and line of scholarship. To accomplish these outcomes, you may have to approve documents for the college's institutional review board (IRB) on human subjects, as well as have clients and legal guardians of clients sign waivers to participate in research and program evaluation, and also allow your clients and staff to be photographed and/or video/audio recorded for research and public relations purposes. Addressing faculty needs for documentation of teaching effectiveness and the need to conduct scholarly projects is critical to successful college-community partnerships. Nonprofit representatives may also be asked by the faculty member to copresent the project at a local, state, national, or international conference, or even be requested to coauthor a journal or magazine article.

Nonprofit organizations can also partner with multiple faculty members on one project in a way that creates interprofessional education opportunities. Cooperation with community partners gives faculty insight into the challenges and needs of the community, but it also allows for joint scholarship. Within the college, interdisciplinary collaborations facilitate scholarship efforts that may not have been pursued otherwise.

One such example is a project developed at the University of Indianapolis several years ago that involved art and theater faculty and students. The focus was on senior citizens and older adults, and on performance and visual art making. But the project took on new dimensions when occupational therapy faculty and students began to study the effects on the participants at the Southeast Senior Center in Fountain Square, Indianapolis. By the end of the one-year project, funded partially through Indiana Campus Compact and the Lily Foundation, Inc., research showed that the participants who worked on a mural painting project using images from their childhood had a greater sense of well-being and a greater sense of community. Originally the art and theater faculty were not trained to conduct the research itself, so the addition of the occupational therapy faculty and students was fortuitous in assessing the impact. Art, theater, and occupational therapy faculty constantly learned new strategies from one another, both in working with community participants and in supervising and inspiring students from other disciplines. The community partner agency benefited as well, as programming for approximately ten of their participants was provided at no cost, and the older adults brought new vitality into the center. Interest in performance created opportunities for students to continue working with a group of senior citizens for additional semesters.

All in all, faculty benefit from these interactions in numerous ways. Besides revitalizing their teaching and providing scholarship opportunities, faculty are also in a position to work outside of the classroom setting. It's an opportunity to try new methods and materials, learn, and use new technologies in new situations. This can have a dynamic impact on the faculty member. For example, during a recent project, faculty at the University of Indianapolis began a digital storytelling project with senior citizens. Working with a student in visual communication design, interviews were videotaped with the first of several participants. From information gathered during the interview session, the faculty member realized a solution to some of the issues with attendance at a regular art class. By working with art students planning the projects, and by interviewing the participants, faculty received new insights into how to conduct the projects to make them more meaningful.

Recognize and Provide Opportunities to Your Faculty Partners
Whatever you do, help faculty help you. Engaged scholars are typically not "me" or "I" kind of people, but they are employed, for the most part, in settings where taking or sharing substantial credit is critical in order to maintain and even increase the flow of time, treasure, and talent to your organization. Help the faculty member play the game that they are in. If the faculty member wins, you win, too, and so do his or her students and your clients!

Nonprofit representatives should be willing to write reference letters for faculty members for promotion, tenure, retention, and posttenure review, as well as nominate them for campus and community awards to bring recognition to the faculty member for his or her efforts. Again, engaged scholars are not "me" people, so they are not going to jump up and say "please nominate me for this award." Nonprofit partners should ask the faculty partner directly if any recognition opportunities are available through the college or through professional associations that the faculty partner would be competitive for. The nonprofit partner should also ask for the faculty partner's vita, curriculum vita, or CV (that's what academics call a resume), as well as a web link to a faculty biography. This will make your job of nominating the faculty member easier when needing to gather information.

A key component to generating recognition for the faculty member and your organization is to be active in soliciting external media coverage from print, broadcast, and online media, as well as internally producing media through self-published online press releases that are intentionally circulated through social media (as highlighted in chapter 3). Often, a good media campaign will lead to recognition for the faculty member and new donors to your organization, as well as assist with annual reporting internally and externally, communicating with stakeholders like your board of directors and donors, and being included in future case expressions and grant proposals. Many successful faculty, especially successful engaged scholars, brand their academic agenda to illustrate the connections between teaching, scholarship, and service through media relations and research (see the Indiana Rural Recreation Development Project at http://www.indstate.edu/inrrdp). Often, good public relations and media coverage lead to recognition for students, faculty, and the agency, and ultimately serve as persuasive artifacts in the on-campus and local community resource allocation processes, as well as in grant funding acquisition. Help faculty help you!

Faculty members could need an array of other things from the partnership that typically would cost your organization little if anything, such as giving the faculty member a title within your organization and documenting that title, the service responsibility, and dates of service on hand-signed letterhead. The faculty members may desire opportunities for more real-world work experience to continue their professional practice in the discipline in which they teach, or they may simply need CEUs to attain or maintain professional certification. They may even desire an opportunity to refine and market their fee-based consulting services.

Nonprofit partners should be willing to serve in a systemic relationship, where you serve on the faculty member's curricular advisory board and the faculty member serves on your board of directors or an advisory committee of some sort (Nickerson, Schaumleffel, & Doyle 2015). Be upfront about what you and your organization want and need from a partnership that will make it worth your time and resource investment, and allow the faculty member to lay his or her cards on the table, too (Schaumleffel, Wilder, & Doyle 2011).

Promotion and Tenure

Although faculty may not initially add a community engagement component to their courses for the sole purpose of career advancement, the reevaluation of existing or developing new courses can result in positive outcomes in this area. Faculty must meet criteria for promotion and tenure, and community engagement courses afford rewards in terms of internal and external recognition. Developing expertise in working with community agencies and developing successful projects that bring positive results (such as determining and meeting community needs, or raising awareness of civic issues) is important to faculty with a community engagement component to their courses.

Rightly or wrongly, while some institutions may not regard Boyer's (1990) scholarship of application/engagement and scholarship of teaching and learning as highly as the scholarship of discovery, there are a growing list of institutions that do. Faculty are also becoming more involved in evaluating student-learning outcomes through assessment, which is an important evaluation tool that helps them gain a better footing for promotion and tenure by systematically improving teaching effectiveness. Other institutions, like those associated with Indiana Campus Compact, see community engagement as vital to the mission and strategic plan of their college. However, that vitality has not trickled down nearly enough from the boards of trustees and senior administration to the tenured faculty, chairpersons, and deans who make critical promotion and tenure decisions (Frank et al. 2011).

Faculty members experience personal growth and often discover inspiration for new teaching strategies through community engagement. This growing and learning process continues throughout their academic life and can lead to new or expanded professional opportunities. Networking, opportunities for scholarship, and possible advancement are other benefits to community engagement for faculty.

Mission Match is the Goal

When project goals are written, the partners should not develop new goals but should find the overlap between their individual existing goals.

It is important for each party to understand the benefits of community engagement for each stakeholder group and how a community engagement project can help them, as well as benefit the other two stakeholder groups. Once each stakeholder understands the benefits to all three groups, those benefits can only be achieved by appreciating the dynamics of a successful community partnership. When the students', organization's, and faculty member's priorities are aligned into equally valued priorities within one project, you have achieved mission match in your partnership. Everyone gets what he or she needs, while working to help the other two groups get what they need. The nonprofit organization helps students and the faculty member. The students help the faculty member and the nonprofit organization. The faculty member helps the students and the nonprofit. Self-interest is always a reliable and reasonable motivator for altruistic community-minded people. There is nothing at all wrong with individuals and organizations helping themselves in the process of helping others.

References

Astin, A. W., and A. L. Antonio. *Assessment for Excellence: The Philosophy and Practice of Assessment and Evaluation in Higher Education.* (Lanham: Rowman & Littlefield Publishers, Inc., 2012).

Bloom, B. S., ed. *Taxonomy of Educational Objectives: The Classification of Educational Goals: handbook I, cognitive domain.* (New York: Longmans, Green, 1956).

Boyer, E. L. *Scholarship Reconsidered: Priorities of the Professoriate.* (Princeton: Carnegie Foundation for the Advancement of Teaching, 1990).

Center for Nonprofit Excellence. (n.d.). *Nonprofit Organizational Assessment.* Retrieved February 14, 2013, from http://www.cnpe.org/sector-insights/osa/

Frank, J. B.; M. Malaby; L. R. Bates; M. Coulter-Kern; S. Fraser-Burgess; J. R. Jamison; L. Stalker-Prokopy; N. A. Schaumleffel.

"Serve at Your Own Risk?: Service-Learning in the Promotion and Tenure Process." *Journal of Community Engagement and Higher Education 1*(2) (2011): 1–13.

Jones, S. R., and K. E. Hill. "Understanding Patterns of Commitment: Student Motivation For Community Service Involvement." *The Journal of Higher Education 74*(5) (2003): 516–539.

Kezar, A., and R. Rhodes. "The Dynamic Tensions of Service-Learning in Higher Education: A Philosophical Perspective." *Journal of Higher Education 72*(2) (2001): 148–71.

Nickerson, Z.; N. A. Schaumleffel; P. R. Doyle. *Making National Nonprofit Partnerships Come Alive at the Local Level: A ScoutReach Laboratory*. Poster presentation to be given at the annual meeting of the Nonprofit Leadership Alliance, Alliance Management/ Leadership Institute, Salt Lake City, UT. January 2015.

O'Meara, K. *Rewarding Faculty Professional Service*, Working paper no. 19. (Boston: New England Resource for Higher Education, 1997).

Schaumleffel, N. A. *Nonprofit Leadership Like it Oughta Be: Normative Perpetual Mission-Focused Experience Management Cycle*. Presentation conducted synchronously online via the High Impact Webinar Series of the Nonprofit Leadership Alliance, Kansas City, MO. February 2014.

Schaumleffel, N. A.; M. Malaby; J. B. Frank. "Risk Management is Not Just for Park and Recreation Professionals Anymore: How to Partner with Faculty on Mutually Beneficial Community Engagement and Service-Learning Projects." *Book of Abstracts: 2010 Indiana Park and Recreation Association State Conference Recreation*

Research Symposium. (Cicero: Indiana Park and Recreation Association, 2010)

Schaumleffel, N. A.; J. Wilder; T. Doyle. The power of strategic partnerships: Fully-integrated American Humanics nonprofit management education program partnerships with ScoutReach, Happiness Bag, Inc., Special Olympics Indiana, the Association of Fundraising Professionals, Autism Speaks U., the ISU Foundation, and e-Tapestry. Paper presented at the annual meeting of the American Humanics Management/ Leadership Institute, Orlando, FL. January 2011.

Simonet, D. *Service-Learning and Academic Success: The Links to Retention Research.* (St. Paul: Minnesota Campus Compact, 2008). Retrieved from http://www.compact.org/wp-content/uploads/resources/downloads/MN-SL_and_academic_success.pdf

Resources

DePauw University Computer Technology Enhancement Program (CTEP) http://www.depauw.edu/offices/ctep/

Hendricks, M.; M. C. Plantz; K. J. Pritchard. "Measuring Outcomes of United Way-Funded Programs: Expectations and Reality." In *Nonprofits and Evaluation: New Directions for Evaluation,* ed. J. G. Carman and K. A. Fredericks. 119: 13–35. (Hoboken, NJ: Wiley InterScience, 2008) DOI: 10.1002/ev Retrieved from http://web.pdx.edu/~stipakb/download/PA555/ OutcomeMeasurementAtUnitedWay.pdf

CHAPTER 5:

How To Get Started with a College and Nonprofit Organization Partnership: Setting Expectations, Networking on Campus, and Managing Student Volunteers

Nathan A. Schaumleffel, PhD, Indiana State University

Nathan D. Mott, MS, MPA, Indiana University-Purdue University Indianapolis

Douglas E. Harms, PhD, DePauw University

Wendy St. Jean, PhD, Purdue University Calumet

One of the most basic functions of youth, human, and social service nonprofit organizations is to truly understand the needs of their constituents. Most organizations struggle with systematically identifying needs. At Indiana State University, over the course of three semesters, we were able to develop an autism-friendly youth organization parents' needs assessment questionnaire for Autism Speaks that was used for a national assessment to guide the development of a publication titled "Leading the Way: Autism-Friendly Youth Organization Guide." The needs assessment revealed that the leading concern of parents of children with autism spectrum disorder in youth recreation settings was staff and volunteer training or lack thereof. This book is being used by scores of youth and family serving organizations

to improve organizational preparedness and staff/volunteer training for providing services to those that struggle with autism spectrum disorder.
—*Dr. Nathan A. Schaumleffel, Autism Speaks volunteer*

Getting Started

College-community partnerships basically start in two simple ways: (1) the faculty or staff member reaches out and asks your organization to work with him or her; or (2) your organization actively seeks out a college faculty or staff member to partner with. Like any relationship that starts and leads to a partnership, we have to first meet, mingle, get acquainted, find common interest, and build trust and respect before one will ask the other to partner.

As faculty and nonprofit leaders build trust and respect and begin discussing a college-community partnership, they should consider developing mutually beneficial community engagement projects—but not necessarily mission-critical projects. Students need to be able to fail without hurting the organization substantially or negatively impacting the organization's clients.

Another discussion point early in the establishment of a college-community partnership is that of sustainability. Funding is often short-term, student and faculty projects are often on a semester timeline, and resources may need to be constantly replenished. These issues are discussed at greater length in chapter 7. For now, keep in mind that sustainability is an issue of great focus for faculty and colleges, so it's a critical element in establishing and maintaining a positive partnership. The building and maintenance of a long-term partnership is worth the effort by both the college and the community partner.

Potential community partners also need to consider the academic calendar when considering partnerships, as well as their expectations for project management and completion. The availability of faculty and students ebbs and flows with very heavy stress times at the beginning and end of each semester due to the academic calendars (i.e., the annual school year schedule). Things like faculty meetings, and preparing course syllabi, and setting up online course websites busy faculty in August and early September, while things like final exams and heavy grading loads fill a professor's time from Thanksgiving to the winter holiday season. As previously mentioned, most professors are on nine or ten month contracts, meaning they are unemployed from mid-May to mid-August. This often means they are unavailable by phone or e-mail, or for meetings, during the summer. Major college calendar events that community partners need to consider when establishing critical dates and timelines are the following: the first day of the semester, homecoming, fall break, Thanksgiving break, study week, final exams, winter break, and spring break. Syncing project timelines with the academic calendar is a key to success in a college-community partnership.

Even though, oftentimes, nonprofit organizations seek college-community partnerships because of the need for or lack of financial resources, consider securing funds to bring to the table. Some colleges want to know that you have a vested interest in a partnership. Having funding can also be a way to get your program moving forward, which could offset the faculty member's time and supplies used for the project.

Excellent college-community partnerships are also built upon three very critical processes: setting your own expectations at an appropriate level, campus networking, and volunteer management.

Set Your Expectations Before Accepting or Seeking a Partnership
So, now, let's get started with actually exploring the partnership process by considering what you should expect when participating in a college-community partnership. The information presented in chapters 1 through 4 is not too good to be true, but you need to have appropriate expectations for timelines, multiple faculty

responsibilities, and, of course, work quality and sometimes behavior of undergraduate students (and even some immature graduate students). It is important to not make assumptions, as well as to not corner the faculty member into overcommitting to your organization and consequently set them up to underdeliver.

In short, you'll also have to consider your expectations and how those expectations put the faculty member on the hook for project completion regardless of student performance. As many of us know, students bring high energy, fresh ideas, and good hearts, but they are not experienced, professional consultants. Also, their follow-through and commitment are not always as good as nonprofit executives and professors expect it should be. Students can be game for new out-of-the-box ideas that the current staff and long-time volunteers are not up for due to too much institutional history and "how we have always done things." Call it coed naivety or youthfulness—whatever you call it, it can be refreshing and it can be frustrating all at the same time.

Be prepared for the bumps. It is often the faculty member's job to protect the students' learning experience, as well as protect the organization's mission, goals, objectives, and their clients' development. This is a precarious position for the faculty member, leaving them open to criticism because they do not necessarily have time to protect themselves. You need to understand that most faculty, if serving as a paid consultant with no responsibility to advance students' learning, would provide world-class, on-time, underbudget consulting to your organization. However, in college-community partnerships they are teaching, serving, and researching. So remember that they are serving your organization and dragging along sometimes thirty to one hundred and fifty students with them, and those students can have issues. You need not be overly judgmental of a faculty member's abilities to complete a task when things go sour. They are trying to move students toward achieving learning outcomes while in the process of serving your organization. Benefit, credit, responsibility, patience, and fault are all three-way streets in these sorts of relationships.

If you want the good and the free that can come from college-community partnerships, as outlined in this book, then you need to be patient with the bumps and frustrations, too. Much of the best learning experiences for the students happen when the project doesn't go as planned. The learning takes time, training, correction, feedback, reflection, and retraining, which is a barrier to project completion from the nonprofit organization's viewpoint. The faculty member has a very difficult job when facilitating these community engagement and service-learning projects if they are to be truly service-learning projects, not just service projects and not just learning projects.

It is also equally important that the students' learning curve not be unethically considered at the expense of the organization's clients, users, participants, or target audience. There is a balance that has to be achieved through negotiation and communication between the main points of contact from the college and the nonprofit organization.

Now, all of that said, let's explore how you go about finding the perfect faculty partner, the mover and shaker that can turn on the faucet of time, treasure, and talent from the local college.

Campus Networking: Finding the Perfect Faculty Partner
Now that you have considered your own expectations for a college-community partnership, it is time to start thinking about how to network on a local college campus. As you can see from chapter 3, colleges have an amazing amount of time, treasure, and talent on campus that can be channeled to your organization if you and your organization have the right relationships across campus. Finding ways to have a continual, sustainable presence on campus, and finding the right go-to person or people on your local campus, are the keys to generating resources for your organization.

Finding the perfect faculty partner takes time, networking, and relationship building!

First and foremost for networking strategy, you'll need to find a way to make at least one new friend in each of the units, divisions, or departments discussed in chapter 3 through on-campus, online, and community networking. You can start by Googling the campus website and searching "service-learning," "civic engagement," or "community service" (e.g., "center for community engagement"). Visiting the college's web page and searching for some of these terms will often lead you to an appropriate contact person. The key is using the buzzwords and office names suggested in chapter 3 to find engaged faculty and staff who would be interested in building a relationship that might grow into a partnership opportunity. Networking with other nonprofit leaders in the community, and specifically asking about the best campus partners, is a fantastic way to grow your list of potential college faculty and staff, too.

As you find each unit, division, or department listed in chapter 3, you should spend time reading the faculty and staff biographies to learn about these folks' experience, interests, and involvement. Many may already have volunteered for your organization, be a current donor, have a child participating at your facility, or have a passion and affinity for your NPO's mission! Many of them can serve in a variety of short- and long-term volunteer roles for your organization. Some will volunteer for one day, others may serve on your board of directors for years. Many will serve in a regular nonboard member role for years if you engage them with your volunteer management skills.

Most university employees are well educated, but they are often strapped with student loan debt and not all that well paid for their education and experience level. This is especially true of young twenty-somethings with their freshly minted PhDs who are seeking tenure, buying their first homes, and starting families. You should engage these folks for time and talent, and not necessarily target them for personal treasure beyond a $25 to $100 annual fund gift. University personnel make excellent advisory committee members (sort of above a casual volunteer but not on the board of directors since leadership giving is often not an option). They will do even more for your organization if you give them a title that will make them look good on campus, especially to the other professors in their department, by attaching their role and title closely to their discipline. This aids their annual review, as well as documents their service each year in a typed letter that is hand signed on your organization's letterhead.

Another simple way of establishing a continual and sustainable presence on campus is through e-newsletter integration, meaning you add all of the key stakeholders from the college campus to your organization's e-newsletter list and ask that all units around campus add you to their e-mail list, list-servs, and e-newsletters.

Also, establishing professional use of social media for your organization and yourself individually and then strategically liking on Facebook and following on Twitter the variety of individual units, departments, colleges, students, staff, faculty, sports teams, fraternities, sororities, coaches, clubs, student newspaper, etc. on campus is absolutely critical to being in the loop to capitalize on a college-community relationship. Nonprofit personnel should exceedingly connect themselves and their agencies to all of the campus social media networks, which are myriad and not necessarily systematically organized, nor university-sponsored. Every student group, athletic or club sports team, fraternity, sorority, residence hall, and faith-based group can quickly create their own Facebook page, Twitter feed, etc. You should connect yourself and your organization via friend requests to all of these social media outlets to keep your fingers on the pulse of campus opportunities.

The next thing you should do is understand mutual reciprocity—that is, simply saying "You scratch my back and I'll scratch yours." One thing you can do is make yourself available for a variety of services, such as being a guest speaker for classes, serving as an internship site supervisor, and attending campus athletic and artistic performances, lectures, and events. You can serve on advisory boards at the university, too. You might even consider eating lunch at the campus's student union or student center, join the campus recreation center as a community member and workout on campus, and even visit the campus library in your free time. Being seen on campus is an important part of channeling college resources to your organization.

The university may offer another opportunity for a nonprofit to get the word out about its services. Do not be shy about asking faculty members or university officials about opportunities to speak on campus, attend meetings, or be added to e-mail and discussion lists. The more a community member is known on campus, the more comfortable campus staff will be with working with him or her and the more aware of campus resources the community member will become.

As your organization starts partnering with college personnel, and after new organizational needs are identified, you should contact previous campus partners with whom you had a positive experience, and describe your ideas for the new project. The faculty member might be interested in partnering with you on this new project, or he or she might be able to suggest other faculty who might be available and interested in partnering with you.

If you had a negative community engagement and service-learning experience with a faculty member, then a final note about perseverance is in order. William Hickson, in 1836, recommended that "if at first you don't succeed, try, try, try again." It's important to keep Hickson's advice in mind when locating a faculty partner. Having a bad experience with one faculty member shouldn't deter you from reaching out to another faculty member, either at that same college or a different one. Persistence is key, and keep in mind that it may take several attempts before finding the perfect faculty partner.

Another suggestion for building your initial campus contacts is to contact organizations that support community engagement and service-learning on college campuses, such as Indiana Campus Compact. Colleges that have community engagement programs are often members of organizations like ICC that support these kinds of activities. Contact a program officer at one of these organizations and describe your project; there's a good chance he or she could get you connected with someone at a local college who could help with your project. Your state's Campus Compact (http://www.compact.org/) may list member colleges in your state and contact information for a faculty liaison, or a person designated as a community engagement leader at the local college.

Community members should also understand the power of being a donor to the college's office of institutional advancement, foundation, sports team, and academic scholarships, even if you have to dip into your own personal pocketbook as opposed to using funds from the organization you represent. But, like a tip at a bar to a bartender, it only counts for faster and preferred service if the bartender sees you put the dollar on the bar or in the jar! The origin of the term tip means "to insure promptness." If the tip is not conspicuous it consequently does no good for insuring promptness. The lesson here is to donate regularly and conspicuously, even if it is not a large monetary donation.

Not all faculty or all disciplines are community focused or community friendly. Pedagogy, also known as a professor's teaching philosophy and style, is deeply rooted in an individual professor as well as disciplinary tradition. Not all faculty and not all disciplines have embraced community engagement, service-learning, and engaged scholarship. If you approach one of these folks about a partnership and get a cold reception, go back to the drawing board and find a better college partner.

Get Volunteer Ready

As you can see, phenomenal opportunities and resources exist on college campuses to help further your organization's mission by channeling time, treasure, and talent from campus to your organization. Opportunities abound through these college-community relationships. However, if you plan to tap into these vast resources it is critical that your organization be college volunteer and resource ready. Have a spectrum of shovel-ready and Internet e-service ready projects at hand, as well as volunteer job descriptions prepared for interested faculty, staff, and students. Your organization needs be volunteer ready and volunteer friendly! You should also have a spectrum of projects and e-projects on hand that have differing levels of associated risk, so that those students with questionable or criminal histories might have an opportunity to contribute at an appropriate level, depending on their transgressions and the amount of elapsed time since their conviction.

If your organization is serious about tapping into college resources, your organization should seriously consider creating a paid position titled Director of Volunteer Management. This can be either a paid full-time or part-time position or even a volunteer position. The director can not only plan projects, and place prepared and responsible volunteers, but he or she can also deal with and triage those college students who show up at the last minute to get in their hours for class. A good volunteer manager can harness the power of last-minute volunteers to benefit the organization.

It would be this person's job to recruit, screen, train, assign, supervise, manage, evaluate, retrain, recognize, and/or even dismiss volunteers, as well as document college-community engagement with your organization (Schaumleffel 2013, 2014). He or she can serve as the internship site supervisor, AmeriCorps Site Supervisor, Federal Work-Study Coordinator, Center for Community Engagement Community Council Representative, etc. The volunteer manager would also be responsible for signing the myriad documents required for students' classes, observations, field work, internships, and volunteer requirements for athletics, Greek Life, etc. Every department tends to have different internship contracts, requirements, reporting procedures and forms, evaluation tools, as well as fraternity, sorority, and athletic community-service forms, Federal Work-Study payroll, etc. One person will need to be the college paperwork expert in your organization to make it easy for you to accept volunteers and for volunteers to choose your organization. In essence, a volunteer manager specializing in college-student service becomes a coprofessor. He or she has a critical role in managing academic dishonesty issues in community engagement and service-learning projects, such as students forging hours or pretending to be someone else.

The volunteer manager should also work to open up all aspects of the organization, including the following: hourly projects, half-day to one-day volunteer opportunities, semester-long internships, allowing college students to attend any and all board meetings, even creating an ex-officio student representative on the organization's board of directors.

This volunteer manager should also work with his or her organization to ensure that engaged students get ample opportunity to become full-time benefits-eligible employees in the organization after graduation. In these cases, it is important to not hold the potential employee's developmental time, learning, and mistakes as a student volunteer against them as a job candidate. The focus of the employee screening process should be on what the person learned as a student, when they made mistakes, grew, and matured, and how they might do things differently given the same situation in the future as a full-time employee.

Once you get a good reputation on campus as a reliable, volunteer-ready, volunteer-friendly community partner, many faculty and staff will seek you and your organization out as a preferred partner for community engagement and service-learning projects.

Volunteer Screening and Criminal Background Checks

Nonprofit organizations must develop, implement, and regularly evaluate a written and board-approved volunteer screening policy for students, faculty, academic staff, and volunteers that are not college affiliated. In the development of this policy, seek advice from legal counsel, criminology professionals, and insurance agents regarding the best, most effective, most efficient, and reasonably priced strategy to get quality criminal background information on each volunteer (Schaumleffel 2003). Without going into great detail here on how to conduct a criminal background check, it is important to realize that every geographic location has different laws based on jurisdiction. There is no one-size-fits-all approach regarding criminal background checks, nor is there any master federal database that has everyone's skeletons neatly logged for a cheap and quick price (Schaumleffel 2003). For long-term volunteers, especially in organizations that serve youth, older adults, or individuals with disabilities, volunteer screening should include a required written application, reference-check phone calls, a face-to-face interview, and an appropriate background check. The background check should include criminal history and may include driving record, financial history, work and volunteer history, etc. Nonprofit organizations need to ask themselves the following questions (Schaumleffel 2003):

- How long and often will a volunteer be at our organization?

- What kinds of risk exist, based on volunteer role (e.g., working with youth, older adults, individuals with disabilities, or finances)?

- How much risk exists?

- What is our budget?

Background checks are an expensive proposition, ranging from roughly $10.00–$150.00 per person depending on the volume of background checks being processed (i.e., economies of scale helps bring down the price per background check), thoroughness, as well as how fast you want the background check completed (Schaumleffel, 2003). In short, the more information and the quicker the turnaround time the more dramatically the price will increase! Remember, you get what you pay for.

What you need to understand is that every college has a different policy about criminal background checks and releasing private information about students to faculty and nonprofit organizations. Federal, state, and local laws govern this process and it is not always easy to know what the college can and can't and will or won't do. Many colleges are downright hypersensitive about protecting students' privacy, even when they push and market community engagement and service-learning to their faculty and students, expecting them to partner with nonprofit organizations. This puts the faculty member in a precarious position, risking inadvertently placing a felon in a volunteer role at an unsuspecting nonprofit organization that works with clients who are often youth, older adults, and individuals with disabilities.

Most colleges do not want to take on the cost of doing background checks or the liability of approving a student as a volunteer for another organization. Often their official stance, although not always a public and open stance, is that volunteer screening is the organization's responsibility, even if students are volunteering as part of a required college-sponsored service-learning course, alternative spring break trip, etc. Many nonprofit organizations blindly assume that college students are OK or have been screened by the college or the professor. It is simply not the case, and nonprofit organizations need to protect their clients, protect their assets, and protect their reputation (Schaumleffel 2003).

When getting started with a college-community partnership, nonprofit leaders need to ensure that they clearly outline who is responsible for volunteer screening, criminal background checks, and the associated cost in a signed memorandum of understanding (see chapter 6 for a discussion of MOUs). Doing the math, a $25.00 background check multiplied by a fifty-student class will cost $1,250.00. Sometimes the expense of criminal background checks is more than the potential return on investment of the students' contribution to the organization.

Special Olympics Indiana has an excellent volunteer screening policy and process. It is written, and board-approved, and integrates a volunteer class system (i.e., Class I and Class II volunteers) based on length of service, unsupervised access to athletes, amount of volunteer training completed, and past criminal history (Schaumleffel 2013, 2014). The Special Olympics Indiana board of directors has also approved and implemented a volunteer criminal history rubric that bans a person, or limits his or her role and access to athletes, based on past criminal conviction and length of elapsed time since the conviction. Special Olympics Indiana demonstrates best practices in volunteer screening and decision making on potential volunteers with criminal histories. They are limiting risk and associated cost with this volunteer class system.

Finally, although not a substitute for the organization's general liability insurance, nonprofit leaders should always encourage volunteers to carry personal liability insurance on themselves as extra precaution in case of a civil lawsuit. Nonprofit organizations also need to explore their insurance coverage (e.g., general liability insurance, directors and officers insurance) when beginning or increasing the use of volunteers.

Volunteer Policies, Training, and Orientation

A critical component to a successful community engagement project is volunteer training. In reality, when partnering with a college you're unlikely to have a faculty member on-site every time and every minute that college students are on-site completing community engagement requirements. Volunteer training for college students is very similar to volunteer training for any population but include the following points of emphasis.

Mission, Core Values, Strategic Plan, Goals, and Objectives. Nonprofit leaders need to train the students in the mission, core values, strategic plan, goals, and objectives of their organization. Students, like any volunteers, conceptually, need, and often want, to understand how the program, project, or service they are involved in contributes to achieving the mission and specific goals and objectives of the organization's strategic plan. When hosting community engagement students, you need to find an effective way to communicate what your organization does and how they will help deliver that program, project, or service.

Designated Leader and Enhanced Communication. You need to communicate who is responsible on-site and who the decision maker is for a variety of issues, including safety, emergency procedures, and organizational policies. The designated leader should be treated and respected in the same way as the professor and should be available by mobile device. It is good planning to also have a designated backup leader. The designated leader and backup leader should define a plan of communication with the faculty member and then train the students on communication procedures. Oftentimes, it can be very beneficial to have two-way radios on-site to communicate while the program, project, or service is underway.

Nonprofit leaders also need to consider the implications of good and bad communication and the impact on relationships between volunteers and staff, as well as student volunteers and regular volunteers. All three stakeholder groups, if led appropriately, can contribute synergistically to the mission, goals, and objectives of the organization. However, conflict between these groups can severely hamper the organization.

Finally, nonprofit leaders should request access to the faculty member's course website via the institution's learning management system (LMS), such as Blackboard or Moodle. Faculty members can arrange for noncollege personnel, such as a community partner, to gain access to the LMS course website by obtaining a user ID and password for the community partner. With a bit of training by the faculty member, the community partner can post relevant information, such as a volunteer policy, training manual and YouTube videos highlighting the organization, as well as post announcements and send e-mail to the entire class. This is a quick and efficient way to change start times or cancel due to weather or other emergencies.

Dress Code and Appearance Policy. First, strongly consider a dress code for student volunteers, as well as policies related to piercings, tattoos, and other appearance issues. It's not likely that students will show up the first day dressed in a toga, however, if your organization's culture requires business casual then you're going to need to define expectations up front. Colleges prepare students to enter a profession; the key word is prepare, as students are not all professionals yet. In fact, community engagement helps students better understand professionalism as it provides an opportunity to work alongside professionals. Faculty will tell you that students are notorious for showing up in shorts, short-shorts, tank tops, halter tops, sagging pants, yoga pants, torn pants, pajama pants, flip-flops, workout clothes, really revealing clothes, skinny jeans, and with body piercings and tattoos. College students also still wear shirts and hats imprinted with alcohol advertisements, marijuana leaves, or with inappropriate words, slogans, images, and innuendos. Many of these fashion styles may not be aligned with your mission and core values as an organization.

When setting a dress code for college-student volunteers, consider the type of work to be done and the existing culture of your organization. Different service projects require different clothing. For example, a site cleanup or Habitat for Humanity build may require closed-toed shoes or boots, jeans, long sleeve shirt, eye protection, and other personal protective equipment. If students will be engaging at a school that has an existing dress code, then ensure the college-student volunteers are aware of the expectations. Believe it or not, some students tend to over-dress, so if you have students working with kids in a gym you many want to give them the heads up and have them not wear a business suit. It's important to communicate and to never as-sume anything.

Mobile Device Usage Policy. Nonprofit leaders should strongly consider a mobile device policy related to personal phone calls; texting; checking e-mail; playing games; taking pictures and videos of staff, volunteers, and clients; posting pictures of staff, volunteers, and clients online; and using social media while on-site. In terms of other social media issues (e.g., Facebook, Twitter, Pinterest, Instagram), nonprofit leaders should strongly consider a social media policy in regard to students friending or following clients and vice versa.

Mobile device and other technology use can be a good thing or it could be a bad thing. A seemingly harmless college student tweet or a Facebook status update might contain damaging, slanderous, or libelous content. There could be a variety of things you may not want them to post, tweet, or capture. Unfortunately, policy or not, it is very difficult to control mobile device and social media use. However, having a written, board-approved policy and training volunteers will help reduce your organization's liability, in some cases, if something goes awry.

The fact of the matter is that mobile technology, connectiv-ity, and social media are not going away. It is quickly and deeply embedding into our culture. College professors have gone from banning technology use in the classroom, to dealing with it, to encouraging it, to requiring it for class. Faculty around the country are learning how to embrace mobile technology in a way that engages the students by using course #hashtags, embedding Twitter in the learning management system, and creating digital storytelling assignments with social media and Storify.

Technology use may or may not have an appropriate place in your organization, making it important to define its appropriate use.

Fraternization Policy. Community partners should also strongly consider a fraternization policy in regard to students and clients who initially meet at the organization and then fraternize outside of the organization. For example, a college student takes a community-based service-learning course and is assigned to complete a project at your organization. The student serves as a math tutor to middle-schoolers. The college student forms a positive mentoring relationship with a middle-schooler, so the child's parent offers to hire the student as an in-home babysitter for pay—outside of the college and outside of your organization. In some instances, if something goes awry or is determined to be illegal, your organization can be held liable for damages.

Conversation and Language Policy. Nonprofit leaders should strongly consider implementing a policy and training related to appropriate conversation, which is a professional skill that many college students need to improve. This is not to say that all students lack this skill, but it's good to define what is expected. It's not just the F-bomb, either. Inappropriate language includes labeling like the r-word or any form of it (i.e., retard, retarded, or any word that ends in "tard"), misusing the word gay (e.g., "that's gay"), using any racial or ethnic slur, using sarcasm, talking about what happened last night, or venting personal opinions. Also, calling adults with disabilities "kids," or referring to older adults as cute can be offensive. Defining appropriate conversation and language, and training students to use them, will limit incidents and conflicts and is key to maintaining an ongoing partnership. Older adults, kids, and individuals with disabilities—in fact, no one—needs or wants to hear about booze, drugs, parties, recreational sex, roommate drama, or strong political opinions.

Logistics and Transportation Issues. Community partners should strongly consider the logistical concerns and transportation issues of their college-student volunteers and clients. It's also important to provide clear directions regarding how to get to a site and how to access the site once there. For example, where do students park, which doors are unlocked, do students need to sign in, will someone escort students into the building, do students need to bring legal identification, who do the students report to once they arrive, and what is the site supervisor's contact information in case they cannot arrive or be punctual?

Food, Beverage, Sanitation, and Personal Articles Policy. Defining a plan for basic human needs is not always an easy task, especially for remote sites, international trips, or construction projects. Even in your local offices and facilities, there can be issues, so it's good to have a plan for food, beverages, and sanitation. Often it is unsanitary or unprofessional to eat or drink during the program, project, or service that is underway. Nonprofit organizations should consider this issue, develop a policy, and train student volunteers.

Organizations may want to designate a safe place for students to keep personal belongings, and provide an overview of the facility, including where restrooms and areas for taking breaks are located. If you are working in remote locations and need volunteers to come equipped with water and a sack lunch, you'll want to communicate the need for the students to come prepared— or you may want to offer to serve meals. Students love pizza or deli sandwiches, but if you do offer a meal, please consider offering vegetarian and vegan options as this is important for some students and faculty. Millennial college students live and eat healthier than past generations, so having fruit, yogurt, and granola available instead of or in addition to bagels and donuts for breakfast is important, too.

Task-Specific Training. Unfortunately, many faculty and community partners don't always do such a great job of task-specific training related to the learning outcomes of the service-learning course and clearly tying the project to the goals and objectives of the organization's mission and strategic plan. Sometimes service-learning is approached from a "plop 'em 'n' flop 'em" perspective, where the professor requires service hours and expects learning to just happen through random experiences.

Every community engagement setting is different; however, think about how your organization would treat a new staff member and apply the same considerations to student volunteers, who need to be effective in achieving learning outcomes and service project goals. The following is an example of task-specific training. The Indiana Department of Natural Resources (IDNR) leads groups of college students in the removal of an invasive plant growing near natural waterways. IDNR staffers spend thirty minutes talking about the effects of the plant and how to effectively remove it. The project involves much more than just pulling weeds, so they take the time to train the students. The task-specific volunteer training helps students see the real-life challenge of biology and organisms in an ecosystem, which allows them to achieve course learning outcomes and service project goals.

Confidentiality and Compliance. For some programs, projects, or services, student volunteers may need access to personal and private information about your organization's clients, participants, or users. It is important to communicate to students that providers in health care and other social services must maintain information in confidence due to laws like the Health Insurance Portability and Accountability Act (HIPAA). Nonprofit leaders need to also understand that, in a similar way, faculty must maintain student privacy and personal information due to laws like the Family Educational Rights and Privacy Act (FERPA). Besides confidentiality issues, it is critical to know and comply with all other relevant federal, state, and local laws.

Mandated Reporting: In most states, mandated reporting is the process of reporting the suspicion of any kind of child abuse or neglect to the state's department of family and child services. Some states have similar laws for older adults and adults with disabilities. In many cases volunteers, including college-student volunteers, in youth, human, and social services organizations—even in a one-day, course-based, service-learning experience—by law are mandated reporters while interacting with your organization's clients. As a nonprofit leader, you need to contact your state's department of family and child services (e.g., Indiana Department of Child Services, Illinois Department of Children and Family Services), learn the laws of your state, and develop an organizational policy regarding mandated reporting by volunteers. Then all volunteers, including student volunteers from college-community partnerships, need to be trained in that policy, which may include how to report on-site incidents and accidents.

Tools, Supplies, Safety Equipment, and First Aid. Tools and supplies are an important topic for any labor force. If you want volunteers to be effective, they need the right tools, supplies, and of course, the right personal protective equipment. Having twenty young college students ready to clean up is great, but if they don't have gloves, rakes, trash bags, soap, water, and first aid supplies it may be difficult to accomplish anything.

Risk Management and Liability. Before partnering with a college, all nonprofit organizations should consider all risk, safety, and liability issues that may affect the partnership, students, faculty, the clients, and the organization. A key role for the memorandum of understanding (MOU), which is discussed at length in

101

chapter 6, is to manage risk and assign responsibility for certain tasks.

As previously mentioned, nonprofit organizations should create and maintain a current volunteer training manual that includes all organizational information, policies, and emergency procedures, such as for weather cancelation, lost clients, and incident response.

International service-learning projects entail a variety of other risks associated with international travel.

Volunteer Evaluation, Recognition, and Reengagement for Curricular and Cocurricular Community Engagement

Volunteer motivation, satisfaction, and recognition are all mission-focused functions for nonprofit leaders. College-student volunteers can be motivated to work hard and do a good job for your organization in a variety of ways, from the altruistic psychological feelings of paying it forward to practical job skill attainment for career development. Also, the benefits of expanding one's professional network and the potential to attain part-time employment while in college, secure an internship, or even postgraduation full-time employment, can and should be motivating factors for student success. Students may also be motivated by the potential to earn academic credit and, simultaneously, a professional reference from their professor and site supervisor for their curricular and cocurricular community engagement. Other potential motivators include being nominated for campus, community, and professional association awards, recognition, and scholarships. In short, self-interest is almost always an excellent motivator of volunteers.

The prospect of earning a college degree and graduating is a major motivator for students, and it is also often in their best self-interest. Nonprofit leaders need to understand that progressive academic credit through community engagement can be just the right carrot to motivate students as they work toward their final, culminating internship (Schaumleffel 2008). In this section, we would like to demystify academic requirements and discuss how nonprofit leaders can assist students in earning a variety of academic credits. It is possible to go beyond the typical, culminating internship experience by engaging students through curricular (e.g., course-based) and cocurricular (e.g., student club) community engagement across all facets of their college careers.

As mentioned in chapter 5, nonprofit leaders in a college-community partnership essentially serve as coprofessors. This means a critical role of the nonprofit leader is to provide verbal and written, constructive, formative and summative feedback to students regarding their performance. This feedback is typically attached to assignment points and has implications for the students' final course grade. Nonprofit leaders will also sign off on the number of hours completed. Preparing for this role is all critical to getting started with a college-community partnership.

Much of this book is related to establishing an initial partnership with a professor for a semester-based community engagement project that will take place within the confines of a single fall or spring college course. Once a professor has a positive relationship with your organization and with you, that professor will likely begin to encourage student community engagement at your organization across all facets of the student experience, from classes to student clubs, to advisement, practicum experiences, additional volunteer work, independent studies, projects, and internships. For example, a student who was required to participate in a project at your organization for a class may continue to volunteer at your site for major-related practicum hours, or encourage fraternity or sorority members to raise money for your organization as a philanthropy project, or complete a final internship at your organization and eventually hire in as a full-time professional.

When getting started with the idea of hosting college interns for a culminating internship experience, nonprofit leaders need to ask themselves if a particular experience is really an internship, or just a singularly focused volunteer experience that you are calling an internship in order to attract a student (Schaumleffel 2008). Internships typically are twelve to sixteen weeks (i.e., a full fall, spring, or summer semester) and require six hundred contact hours or more of on-site time. This averages out to forty hours per week. Internships are typically best when the student is not taking classes on-campus or online simultaneously. Be aware that some majors do not require an internship, and for the majors that do require an internship there are a variety of requirements, number of hours, evaluation styles, reporting requirements, and faculty site-visit policies. For all of these reasons, we encourage you to heed our advice regarding creating a position of Director of Volunteer Management.

Internship job descriptions should be written for different majors and target mission-focused projects that achieve the learning outcomes and professional competencies of each specific major (Schaumleffel 2008). For example, recreation majors need a management internship and should not serve as a camp counselor or lifeguard (Schaumleffel 2008). Child development majors need to have responsibilities and substantial contact with youth and families, not to work primarily alongside an administrative assistant in a youth-serving organization (Schaumleffel 2008). Nonprofit management majors need to work on fundraising, volunteer management, and program evaluation, not to teach swim lessons at a nonprofit camp (Schaumleffel 2008).

Culminating internships for a returning student volunteer or staff member need to provide different and more advanced meaningful experiences with more responsibility (Schaumleffel 2008). Nonprofit leaders need to understand that taking on an intern requires time to mentor, guide, assist, provide feedback, and evaluate on a regular, formative timeline. Interns can take work off of your plate, but that plate will be filled up again by the student-development responsibilities of being an internship supervisor—remember that you're effectively a coprofessor (Schaumleffel 2008). Interns are not capable, autonomous professionals, they are chicks who need to be taken under your wing, and that takes your time (Schaumleffel 2008).

Unfortunately, way too many nonprofit organizations that are short on cash and short on staff call every position an internship, even when it's not. More alarming is the fact that there is little to no supervision, much less qualified supervision, by an on-site internship supervisor (Schaumleffel 2008). Interns are not free staff nor indentured servants (Schaumleffel 2008).

Internships are a three-way learning community between the student, internship site supervisor (i.e., you), and the faculty member (Schaumleffel, 2008). Culminating internships should have project requirements that test skills, allow students to struggle—sometimes even fail—then reflect and improve, all under the supportive guidance of an internship site supervisor and a professor (Schaumleffel 2008). Internships should include professional networking opportunities, relevant certification training opportunities, skill expansion, confidence building, and should have plentiful opportunities to construct artifacts related to professional competencies for the students' professional portfolio and resume (Schaumleffel 2008). Interns should have opportunities to tie theory to practice and see best practices modeled in the community setting (Schaumleffel 2008). Internships need to be well planned and goal oriented, with SMART objectives (i.e., specific, measurable, achievable, realistic, and with a timetable) in terms of projects that meet learning outcomes that are challenging, achievable, and achieve higher levels of learning on Bloom's (1956) taxonomy of learning objectives (e.g., analysis, synthesis, and evaluation), as well as aligned with strategic goals and objectives of the organization (Schaumleffel 2008). Internships are still a class with a professor and assignments. Students and site supervisors often forget the academic component of the experience is as important as getting hours completed (Schaumleffel 2008).

In most cases, internships can be paid or unpaid (Schaumleffel 2008). If an internship has mission-critical job functions in it, then it is absolutely critical to find the right intern who will be successful. In these cases, the old adage still holds true, you often get what you pay for. The best students often want, need, and even expect to be paid for serving as an intern, unless you can recruit them with other carrots that are in their best interests (Schaumleffel 2008). Recruiting an intern at the last minute will most likely reap an unqualified, underprepared student, making the experiences negative for both you and the student (Schaumleffel 2008). The best college students have internships lined up at least one or one-and-a half semesters ahead of time (Schaumleffel 2008). This means the typical summer intern starting on May 15 was recruited, screened, approved, and accepted by October 15 of the previous year.

The keys to quality internship experiences for a nonprofit organization are for nonprofit leaders to have:

- a positive, long-term relationship with faculty;

- developmental community engagement opportunities in place at the agency (course-based service-learning, practicum opportunities, summer employment, independent studies or projects, internships);

- internship opportunities year round, not just in summer (Schaumleffel 2008).

Just Say No If You Need To—It's OK, Really!

The focus of this chapter has been on getting started. But, as previously mentioned, college-community partnerships are initiated in two ways—by the nonprofit leader or by the college or a specific professor. Sometimes you may not be ready to get started when approached by a college or a faculty member, and that is OK!

There may well be times when a faculty member approaches you with a proposal for partnering and, for whatever reason, you might prefer not to take on a partner right then. Perhaps you don't have the time or resources to commit to the partnership, or the project isn't something you need at the time, or you've had a bad experience with the faculty member in the past; there are a host of reasons. In these situations it is OK to say "No"! It's important to understand that community engagement partnerships must be collaborative and beneficial to *all* parties involved—you, your organization, the faculty member, the college, and the students. If the proposed partnership is not beneficial or workable for you and your organization, then it would not benefit anyone to pursue it. Saying no is the honest and appropriate response.

If you do say no, you should be honest with the faculty member and explain your reasons. If this is not the right time for the partnership, explain this so the faculty member knows that a future partnership is not out of the question. If your past experience has been problematic, letting the faculty member know this could help him or her address the problems and concerns you have. If the proposed project doesn't match your needs, letting the faculty member know could help him or her develop a more appropriate and beneficial proposal in the future that will achieve mission match by aligning with your organization's mission and strategic plan. Keeping the lines of communication open between you and the college could provide significant benefits in the future, so be sure to explain why you're saying no. Maybe you just mean "Not right now."

References

Bloom, B. S., ed. *Taxonomy of Educational Objectives: The Classification of Educational Goals: handbook I, cognitive domain.* (New York: Longmans, Green, 1956).

Hickson, W. E. *The Singing Master.* (Woodbridge, UK: Boethius Press, 1836).

Schaumleffel, N. A. *Developing information infrastructure: Improving youth-serving agencies' ability to conduct efficient, comprehensive, and cost-effective criminal background checks on staff and volunteers.* Presentation to Public Policy Committee of the Champaign County YMCA, Champaign, IL. July 2003.

Schaumleffel, N. A. *Campademics: So you want college interns?* Presentation conducted at the annual meeting of the American Camp Association, Nashville, TN. February 2008.

Schaumleffel, N. A. *Evaluating volunteers.* Presentation and round-table discussion facilitated at the annual meeting of the Indiana

Youth Institute Because Kids Count State Conference, Indianapolis, IN. December 2013.

Schaumleffel, N. A. *Volunteers—Plaque 'Em & Sack 'Em: Managing Risk and Mission-Focus in Nonprofit and Public Recreation Agencies.* Presentation conducted at the annual Allen Symposium of the Department of Health Education and Recreation, Southern Illinois University Carbondale, Carbondale, IL. April 2014.

Resources

Campus Compact
http://www.compact.org/

CHAPTER 6:

The Nuts and Bolts of College and Nonprofit Organization Partnerships: Memorandums of Understanding

Nathan A. Schaumleffel, PhD, Indiana State University

Douglas E. Harms, PhD, DePauw University

Nathan D. Mott, MS, MPA, Indiana University-Purdue University Indianapolis

Wendy St. Jean, PhD, Purdue University Calumet

Since many senior citizens benefit by interacting with pre–art therapy students through arts programming, a partnership between the University of Indianapolis and an assisted living facility is an excellent fit. The immersion experience brings students much needed real-life experience to prepare for graduate school, resulting, too, in more socially engaged senior citizens with an increased sense of community and well-being. One senior citizen, formerly withdrawn and nonresponsive, reminds us of the importance of sustaining the partnership by asking daily, as the semester comes to an end, "when will the college students be coming back?"
—Marilyn Lake McElwain, Service-learning in the Arts

So far, we have shared why partnering with a college for community engagement projects is a good idea and a good investment for your organization. We then gave very tangible ideas on what time, treasure, and talent are available from a college if you find the right movers and shakers on campus. We spent some time exploring why faculty and students would work free of charge or below market value to help your organization achieve its mission, as well as explaining what you should expect when participating in a college-community partnership. We also spent some time discussing how to get started and get volunteer ready. If this all still sounds good to you, then let us now explore how to actually get started in building relationships with faculty and staff, so that impactful partnerships may begin to develop and bear fruit. The nuts and bolts of college-community partnerships, which also create the foundation of excellent partnerships, are thoughtful and well-written memorandums of understanding.

Once a community partner has been identified and a collaborative relationship has been firmly established, then discussions that lead to choosing a project can begin. These discussions must include honest conversations about goals, objectives, needs, resources, and timelines. Partnerships require clearly stated roles, responsibilities, resource allocations, and outcomes (BoardSource n.d.). The results of these conversations should lead to a memorandum of understanding (MOU) for your college-community partnership.

An MOU is a written document used to connect two organizations around a task or a project. An "MOU is an agreement between parties that outlines the roles, responsibilities, services to be provided and expected outcomes" (Eisenhauer, Marthakis, Jamison, & Mattson 2011, 170). Having an MOU provides structure to the partnership, as well as some level of protection for all parties by clearly outlining responsibilities. MOUs are also sometimes called partnership agreements, project outlines, project proposals, and project scope descriptions. Sometimes the word "contract" is used, but that is typically a legally loaded word and should be avoided in most cases.

MOUs put partnerships on paper by writing down who is going to do what and when it is going to be done. MOUs enhance communication, limit conflict, and hold all stakeholders accountable.

MOUs do not have to be complicated. They exist on a spectrum from very simple one-page documents to long, complicated agreements. Whatever the length, the executive director of the nonprofit organization should always be involved in the process of developing the MOU. The executive director and/or board president/chairperson will determine if board approval is needed before it is signed. The partnering faculty member should also know, per his or her college's policy, who is allowed to sign the MOU for the college. In many cases, an MOU for community engagement projects conducted in a class may need to be signed on behalf of the college by a higher ranking administrator, such as a department chairperson, dean, or vice president, not just the faculty member. Few faculty have the ability to commit the university in a binding legal document, however, there is generally an established process for this at each college.

The first step in establishing an MOU is being upfront (i.e., laying your cards on the table early and fully) about what you and your organization want and need from a partnership for it to be worth your resource investment (Schaumleffel, Wilder, & Doyle 2011). As previously discussed, the faculty member's professional needs should be considered at this time and included in the MOU. Then, strict and specific identification of what each party has to offer and what each party expects is key. An MOU should include the following sections:

- Mission of the college and nonprofit organization

- Description of project, program, or service

- Goals and objectives of agency, students (i.e., learning outcomes and professional competencies), and faculty member

- Needs of agency, students, and faculty member

- Risk and liability analysis

- Roles and responsibilities of agency, students, and faculty member

- Expected outcomes, deliverables, and/or services to be provided by agency, students, and faculty member

- Project timeline with specific deadlines

- Resources to be provided by the agency, students, and faculty member

- Financial considerations

- Formative evaluation of partnership process

- Summative evaluation of partnership process

- Dissolution plan

- Intellectual property ownership (if applicable)

- Contact information for the main point of contact for the agency and the faculty member

- Signatures of appropriate college and nonprofit organization representatives

Now that we have outlined the main sections of a college-community partnership memorandum of understanding, let's take a brief looks at each section individually.

Mission of the College and Nonprofit Organization

This section clearly identifies the mission statement of both the college and the nonprofit organization, and clearly identifies the overlap in mission in articulating that a partnership between the two institutions has merit for mission match.

Description of Project, Program, or Service

This section clearly provides a project overview that considers some basic logistics, like facility space, and the minimum and maximum number of students if your project is going to be a meaningful learning experience (please note that many classes enroll over fifty students). You'll also need to consider whether your project is a one-day service project, a semester-long technical assistance or consulting project, or somewhere in the middle. One project may also cut across multiple courses in one semester or one or more classes across multiple semesters and multiple academic years.

Goals and Objectives of Agency, Students (i.e., Learning Outcomes and Professional Competencies), and Faculty Member

This section identifies the goals and objectives of each stakeholder. The goals and objectives should be clearly written in SMART format (i.e., specific, measurable, achievable, realistic, and with a timetable). The goals of the project intended for student learning and professional competence should be written by the faculty member as learning outcomes/objectives, because assessment of learning will take place in the Formative and Summative Evaluation of Partnership Process sections of the MOU. Student-learning outcomes should come directly from a well-written course syllabus that is aligned with a curricular assessment plan. The project, program, and service goals and objectives of a nonprofit organization should come directly from the program evaluation logic model, which is aligned with the mission and strategic plan of the organization.

Needs of Agency, Students, and Faculty Member
This section clearly identifies the self-interest of each stakeholder in the partnership (i.e., laying your cards on the table). You can acquire human, financial, and in-kind resources, including technical expertise, for your overburdened nonprofit organization to meet community needs—all and often entirely free of charge. But before you contact a local college, make sure you spend time defining your needs and the scope of specific projects.

Risk and Liability Analysis
This section comprehensively analyzes the risk associated with a specific community engagement project, program, or service. Risk management is critically important to all colleges and, likewise, it should be a primary concern for all nonprofit organizations. Many colleges require faculty members to conduct a risk analysis of their community engagement projects or program proposals.

Risk is defined as the potential to lose something of value (Tholkes 1998). A risk analysis clearly identifies any potential risk (i.e., objective, calculated, perceived, reckless) associated with the proposed project or program with strategies to mitigate the risk (Tholkes 1998). As written in *On the Guard II: The YMCA Lifeguard Manual* (1997), risk management is an effort to safeguard against negligent acts and to provide an environment that is reasonably free from hazards by following best practices in the supervision of participants, observation and maintenance of indoor and outdoor environmental conditions, and the manner in which activities are conducted. Risk management strategies (i.e., avoidance, modification, retention, sharing), as outlined by the Nonprofit Risk Management Center (n.d.), should be considered and identified. Any risk, safety, and liability management responsibilities identified from the risk analysis (including logistical considerations and the person or position responsible for volunteer screening and criminal background checks as well as the associated cost) should be outlined in the roles and responsibilities of the nonprofit organization, students, and faculty member section of the MOU.

When assessing potential risks of community engagement activities, colleges may need to answer the following questions: What are the potential risks to students from interacting with the agency's clients? What are the potential risks to the agency's clients and staff from interacting with students? What are the potential risks to students as they travel to and from the agency? How is risk and/or liability insurance provided to cover students? How is the confidentiality of staff, clients, and students assured? Should students and faculty purchase personal liability insurance?

As the college analyzes potential risks they may ask you to complete a self-assessment of risk and/or they may have conversations with you about risks. Some of the questions you may need to answer could be the following: How will your staff supervise students while they're on-site, and how many students will be supervised at one time? Will students be working with behaviorally challenged individuals, individuals with a known criminal or violent background, or unsupervised minors? Is the worksite considered to be in a high crime area? Will students be required to work at night, and if so will staff be present? Are there concerns with security at the site? Have there been any incidents of criminal activity at the site? Are there any hazards at the site that could harm students? Will students be working with hazardous materials or heavy equipment? Do you provide safety orientation for students? Does your site have an emergency plan, and are all exits adequately marked? Does your organization carry liability or other kinds of insurance that covers students? Are students allowed to take photos or video? Will your organization take photos or videos of the students?

Some of these conversations can be difficult and perhaps uncomfortable, but keep in mind that risk management aims to identify, evaluate, and minimize risk to students, the college, your clients, your organization, and the faculty partner. Spending time up front analyzing potential risks will result in a safer experience for everyone involved. Most colleges have an Office of Risk Management, so it would behoove the faculty partner to work with this office to develop the risk analysis section of the MOU.

If the proposed community engagement project includes data collection on human subjects, then the faculty partner will need to submit a project proposal to the college's institutional review board (IRB) for approval. This process can be cumbersome and time-consuming, and it may directly impact the project timeline and specific deadlines. IRB approval, in essence, is part of the risk and liability analysis.

Roles and Responsibilities of Agency, Students, and Faculty Member

This section clearly identifies who is responsible for which specific tasks. It should also clearly identify logistical considerations; who is responsible for volunteer screening and criminal background checks and the associated cost; and any risk, safety, and liability management responsibilities. It is critical to align your needs and desired projects to the learning outcomes of the students and the professional-development needs of the faculty partner. This section may include information regarding how each stakeholder (i.e., agency, students, and faculty) will help the other two stakeholders meet their identified goals, objectives, and needs through collaborative support.

Expected Outcomes, Deliverables, and/or Services to be Provided by the Agency, Students, and Faculty Members

This section specifically identifies and describes (i.e., provides the format for) the expected outcomes, deliverables, and or services to be provided by each stakeholder. In short, this section identifies who is going to do what.

When producing the MOU, all project partners, but especially faculty members, should make a concerted effort to undercommit and overdeliver by conservatively predicting what they can realistically achieve while managing a partnership and increasing student learning through substantial individual, small group, and classwide reflection of experiential education learning activities. It is critical when outlining outcomes, deliverables, and/or services that expectations of work quality are clearly articulated with the community partner, especially when working with undergraduate students. Oftentimes, community partners can forget that students are learning and are not consulting experts.

Project Timeline with Specific Deadlines
This section builds upon the expected outcomes, deliverables, and/or services section of who is going to do what by adding the when. When establishing a project with timelines, realistic logistics need to be considered. For example, project timelines in a community agency need to take into account the university/school calendar, such as fall and spring break, study weeks, and final exams. Logistical considerations like transporting students to project sites are critical. When developing the MOU, partners should consider other logistical and social issues like meals, finance, parental support, and socioeconomic issues.

Resources to be Provided by the Agency, Students, and Faculty Member
This section identifies, in bulleted format, what specific resources will be provided by each stakeholder.

Financial Considerations
This section should clearly identify issues related to payments, stipends, expenses (including the associated cost of background checks), and/or fees for service. It is often helpful to attach a project

or program budget in line-item format that financially details the MOU. MOUs and budgets can be created in many different formats, but typically the nonprofit leader can allow the college's Office of Sponsored Programs or Office of Grants and Contracts to draft the MOU and the project/program budget. Some budgets designate faculty time, summertime pay rate, and fringe benefits, as well as matching funds. Other line items may be for other staff time, supplies, transportation, meals, student hourly pay, student fees, and equipment. Many colleges may differ in how they treat or differentiate the resources.

Although the focus of this book has primarily been on acquiring time, treasure, and talent from a college free of charge, there are times when the nonprofit organization will have to contribute money to the student project. When planning a project, it is important to talk about the supplies that are needed, how they will be secured, and who will secure them.

Aside from the realization that projects may involve materials costs (e.g., rakes, paint, software), students sometimes will need a stipend if the project is to be sustained over a long period of time. One example is student tutors. Programs exist wherein schools can get college students as tutors for only a fraction of the market price. However, because it is critically important that the students show up on a regular basis, they need a stipend to give them the motivation to prioritize this commitment over other competing commitments in their lives. When a project is mission-critical, consider generating some funds for student stipends.

Formative Evaluation of Partnership Process

This section should identify a periodic check-in process to evaluate the progress of the expectations and deliverables of the partnership, as well as the achievement of the goals and objectives of the agency, students, and faculty member. The goals of the project intended for student learning and professional competence (i.e., learning outcomes/objectives) should be formatively assessed by the faculty member and shared with the nonprofit partner.

If the formative evaluation process determines the partnership is progressing positively and that the goals and objectives of the agency, students, and faculty member are being achieved, the stakeholders should consider leveraging public and media relations to publicize their success internally to the college and nonprofit organization, as well as externally to the general public.

Summative Evaluation of Partnership Process
This section should identify a final evaluation process to assess the expectations and deliverables of the partnership, as well as the achievement of the goals and objectives of the agency, students, and faculty member. The goals of the project intended for student learning and professional competence (i.e., learning outcomes/ objectives) should be summatively assessed by the faculty member and shared with the nonprofit partner. Also, the strengths, weaknesses, and future of the partnership should be assessed, as well as the sustainability and leadership succession planning. The summative evaluation should provide each stakeholder the opportunity to measure the return on investment (ROI) from the partnership.

If the summative evaluation process determines the partnership concluded positively and substantial goals and objectives of the agency, students, and faculty member were achieved, the stakeholders are strongly encouraged to leverage public and media relations to publicize their success internally to the college and nonprofit organization, as well as externally to the general public.

Furthermore, nonprofit leaders should plan to work with their faculty partners to develop means of disseminating the results of the project, which may be through reports to the board of directors, peer-reviewed scientific journal articles, scholarly conference presentations, community summit presentations, etc. Both sides of the partnership should work to ensure that the presentation and publication of project results inform future actions and projects implemented by the partners, together or separately.

Dissolution Plan

This section identifies a specific process for ending the partnership before the project is complete or at the completion of the project, program, or service. It is critical for the faculty partner to ensure that the project dissolution timeline is enforced in a positive way, so that he or she is not still on the hook to fix or finish the student project for the agency as a free consultant long after students have received their grades and have mentally disengaged from the project. The dissolution plan should be an "out" for the faculty member or nonprofit organization in the event that the project or program goes awry. More importantly, the dissolution plan, if done positively, should contribute to the sustainability of the project or program and maintain positive relationships, as well as sustain the benefits that accrued from the project, program, or service.

Intellectual Property Ownership (if applicable)

This section should include a clause regarding data collection, data ownership, and right to publish and present information from the project. Ownership of images, photos, and audio or video recordings should also be addressed.

Contact Information for the Main Point of Contact for the Agency and the Faculty Member

This section should provide the full contact information for the main point of contact of the nonprofit organization and the faculty member of the college including the following: name, street address, city, state, zip code, phone number, fax number, e-mail address, and organizational website address. Contact information may also include Facebook name, Twitter handle, Skype ID, and any other relevant social media information that might be useful for electronic communication, web conferencing, and public relations.

Signatures of Appropriate College and Nonprofit Organization Representative that has Signatory Authority

This section should provide a signature line for each appropriate college and nonprofit organization representative who has signatory authority, as well as provide the full contact information for each signatory, including the following: name, street address, city, state, zip code, phone number, fax number, e-mail address, and organizational website address. Each signatory may or may not be the main point of contact for the project or program implementation. Few faculty have the ability to commit the college in a binding legal document.

References

BoardSource. *Partnerships.* Retrieved December 1, 2010, from http://www.boardsource.org/Spotlight.asp?ID=116.375

Eisenhauer, M. J.; N. B. Marthakis; J. Jamison; M. Mattson, eds. (2011). *Charting the Course for Service-Learning: From Curriculum Considerations to Advocacy—A Faculty Development Workbook.* (Indianapolis: Indiana Campus Compact, 2011).

Nonprofit Risk Management Center. *Basic risk management: Four Risk Management Techniques.* Retrieved May 6, 2014, from http://www.nonprofitrisk.org/tools/basic-risk/3.shtml

On the Guard II: The YMCA Lifeguard Manual 3rd ed. (Champaign: Human Kinetics, 1997).

Schaumleffel, N. A.; J. Wilder; T. Doyle. The power of strategic partnerships: Fully-integrated American Humanics nonprofit management education program partnerships with ScoutReach, Happiness Bag, Inc., Special Olympics Indiana, the Association of Fundraising Professionals, Autism Speaks U., the ISU Foundation, and e-Tapestry. Paper presented at the annual meeting of the American Humanics Management/ Leadership Institute, Orlando, FL. January 2011.

Tholkes, B. F. "Defining risk." *Camping Magazine, 71*(5) (1998): 24–26.

Resources
Nonprofit Risk Management Center: Volunteer Risk Management Tutorial
http://www.nonprofitrisk.org/tools/volunteer/volunteer.shtml

CHAPTER 7:
Ethical Issues with College and Nonprofit Organization Partnerships

Tina M. Kruger, PhD, Indiana State University

Douglas E. Harms, PhD, DePauw University

Nathan A. Schaumleffel, PhD, Indiana State University

In January 2010, while leading a winter-term in-service (WTIS) trip to El Salvador, I was struck by how much impact long-term relationships between partners can have on communities. My students and I had been working in the community of Santa Marta, but we spent one weekend in Suchitoto to attend the annual music and arts festival celebrating the signing of the 1992 Peace Accords. Over the years several DePauw WTIS teams had worked in Suchitoto, building the amphitheater where the festival took place. Every hour or so the announcer would thank DePauw University for building the facilities. Over the course of the weekend hundreds of people whom we had never met approached us to thank us. Neither I nor anyone on my team had played any role in the construction of the amphitheater, and I was embarrassed to receive their gratitude; however I was overwhelmed to see the profound impact WTIS teams had on the people of Suchitoto.

—Dr. Douglas E. Harms, Winter Term in Service

In chapter 6, in the outline for what should be included in a memorandum of understanding (MOU), we spent some time discussing intellectual property ownership. Intellectual property (IP) often develops during community engagement projects from data-collection type projects that might include research studies, needs assessments, program evaluations, site observations, focus groups, and surveys among others. As previously mentioned, faculty must not only teach students and provide service to community organizations, but they must also create scholarly products in many forms including peer-reviewed published research studies and conference presentations. IP can also include images, photos, and audio and video recordings.

Considering the faculty member's need to publish and present his or her engaged scholarship work, it is critical that the MOU allows the faculty member to maintain sole or at least equal rights to any data produced from a community engagement project. If you work with a faculty partner in this way, you will get more from the faculty partner and the college in terms of time, treasure, and talent.

Oftentimes the data collected from a project can also be used to meet a goal and objective of the nonprofit organization. For example, a needs-assessment report, which could be used to determine programs and services to be offered in the future, or a program evaluation report, which could be used for improved management of organizational resources and reporting to external funders like the United Way, foundations, and private donors.

If you approach a faculty member to conduct a community engagement project in your agency that collects any kind of data from humans of any age to be used for any purpose, which includes needs assessments, program evaluations, or client satisfaction surveys, the faculty member will be expected to submit the research and data-collection proposal to the college's institutional review board (IRB). On some campuses the IRB is also known as the human subjects committee.

When constructing an MOU for a college-community partnership that includes a project with some form of data collection from human subjects, the following sections of the MOU may be heavily, or only slightly, impacted:

- Description of project, program, or service

- Goals and objectives of agency, students (i.e., learning outcomes and professional competencies), and faculty member

- Needs of agency, students, and faculty member

- **Risk and liability analysis**

- Roles and responsibilities of agency, students, and faculty member

- Expected outcomes, deliverables, and/or services to be provided by agency, students, and faculty member

- **Project timeline with specific deadlines**

- Resources to be provided by the agency, students, and faculty member

- Financial considerations

- **Intellectual property ownership**

Nonprofit partners should recognize that the MOU will be significantly impacted in the sections regarding risk and liability analysis, project timeline with specific deadlines, and intellectual property ownership if data is collected.

Faculty members must submit data collection project proposals to the college's IRB to gain approval to collect data from human subjects. Nonprofit partners also need to understand that if they want free services related to research studies, needs assessments, program evaluation, and client satisfaction surveys that they will need to be extremely patient with the faculty member and college.

Sometimes nonprofit leaders approach a faculty member about launching a data-collection type of community engagement project on a very short timeline, the same semester even. In most cases, a compressed timeline for these projects is just not possible. The message here is if you need data collected and analyses completed with human subjects, then you need to give the faculty member at least two semesters lead time, which is almost a full calendar year.

Gaining a determination for a project via IRB can be very time-consuming and cumbersome for the faculty member. It takes away from other parts of his or her job, including other research and scholarship projects, to provide this service to your nonprofit organization. Considering the effort it takes to gain approval for these sorts of projects, it is absolutely critical that intellectual property ownership issues are outlined in the MOU, so that the faculty member can get scholarship needs met from the partnership.

Now that you have a better idea of issues surrounding faculty scholarship responsibilities, intellectual property ownership, and the risk associated with data collection from human subjects, let's now discuss IRBs and why they matter. After a discussion on IRBs, we will review issues related to ethics in community-based participatory research emphasizing sustainability of projects, programs, and services, as well as nonprofit management ethics related to program evaluation, fundraising, and volunteer management.

Institutional Review Boards and Community Engagement Projects: What is IRB and Why Does it Matter?

As introduced above, the faculty partner on your project may want to collect data during the project to be used in his or her professional research program. Typically, when research activities involve human subjects, federal regulation requires the researcher to have the project reviewed by an institutional review board, affectionately called an IRB. Every college has an IRB, and although the specific process varies somewhat from institution to institution, the purpose and intent of the IRB is the same.

The purpose of the IRB is to protect the human subjects who are participating in the research, especially those persons who belong to a special or protected population. This would include participants under eighteen years of age, prisoners, inpatients and outpatients, individuals with intellectual or physical disabilities, or pregnant women. IRBs evaluate the degree of risk to the participants—including potential physical, psychological, or social harm or invasion of privacy—and the potential benefit (if any) the participant (or the community) might receive from the research. IRBs generally require that participants be well informed about the purpose of research and fully understand the procedures involved so they may appreciate any potential risks and benefits. Participants must voluntarily consent to participate, and minors typically must assent to participate. Of special note is the fact that persons under eighteen years of age are a protected population. Informed consent must be given by the minor's legal parent or guardian and the minor must also assent to participate. In short, even if a parent or guardian gives consent for his or her child to participate, the child can choose not to participate.

The IRB policies at colleges are basically derived from federal regulations. Specifically, IRBs are guided by the Code of Federal Regulations 45 CFR 46: Public Welfare and Protection of Human Subjects (US Department of Health and Human Services

(USDHHS 2014). When a faculty member enters into a partnership with a nonprofit organization to conduct a community engagement project that includes data collection from human subjects, possibly in the form of research studies, needs assessments, program evaluations, site observations, focus groups, and surveys, among others, the faculty member needs to determine if the project is subject to IRB review based on his or her college's policies and procedures. The faculty member may need to consult with colleagues, department chairperson, and members of the IRB on his or her campus.

The federal government, through the USDHHS (2014), defines human subjects as "a living individual about whom an investigator (whether professional or student) conducting research obtains: (a) data through intervention or interaction with the individual; or (b) identifiable private information." It goes on to define research as "a systematic investigation designed to contribute to generalizable knowledge." Although nonprofit organization clients or participants are definitely human subjects when data is collected from them, many community engagement projects (e.g., needs assessment, program evaluation) that collect data are not attempting to contribute to generalizable knowledge, thus often making a community engagement project exempt from continuing IRB oversight. Only the IRB can determine that a data-collection project meets the criteria necessary for an exempt determination.

Dr. Kimberly Bodey, Vice Chair of the Indiana State University Institutional Review Board, makes the absolutely critical point that "...even if data-collection activities do not meet the federal definition of research with human subjects, we still have an ethical responsibility related to the Belmont principles: respect, beneficence, and justice." Respect is embodied in the informed consent process and in regard for privacy. Beneficence takes the form of competent researchers, quality research design, and favorable risk-benefit analysis. Justice involves the equitable distribution of benefits and burdens of the research.

As previously mentioned, the IRB process can be quite cumbersome and involved, and it often takes a significant amount of time to get an IRB determination for a project, depending on the complexity and level of risk of the proposed data collection. The researcher cannot begin gathering data until a final written IRB determination is received, and this can potentially delay the start of the project.

For the most part, understanding the IRB process and getting an IRB determination is the responsibility of the faculty member, though you may be involved with some aspects of the process. The main point here is that the IRB process can impact timing of the project and must be taken into consideration when developing timelines and procedures.

Nonprofit organizations need to determine when they are subject to federal regulations related to human subjects whether in a partnership with a college or not. According to the National Research Act of 1974, any agency receiving federal funds must comply with federal guidelines regarding human subjects. So, nonprofit organizations receiving funding for projects, programs, and services that include data collection from human subjects, such as federally mandated program evaluation for Twenty-First-Century Community Learning Center grants, likely need to comply. Nonprofit leaders, if receiving federal funds for a project, program, or service, and seeking out a community engagement partnership with a college to conduct some sort of data collection, should absolutely disclose this information to the faculty member, so that they can review federal policy with his or her department chairperson, dean, and the IRB. Nonprofit leaders should also confer with the grant officer that oversees their federal grant regarding the need for IRB review for human subjects protection and compliance.

Also, not all projects need an IRB review. The faculty member will have to work with his or her IRB in determining whether or not the proposed project requires IRB review. For an example of an IRB policy, visit DePauw University's IRB Policy at

http://www.depauw.edu/offices/academic-affairs/ human-participants-and-animal-use/guidelines-for-using-human-sub/

Applying Community-Based Participatory Research Principles to College and Nonprofit Organization Partnerships
Given a history of human rights abuses (e.g., the Tuskegee Syphilis Study, Milgram Obedience Experiment, Stanford Prison Experiment), academic researchers often face big challenges in working with their target communities and nonprofit partners. In response to both the abuses and challenges in college-community partnerships, a framework for conducting research ethically and sustainably in such partnerships was created and titled community-based participatory research, also known as CBPR (Israel, Schulz, Parker, Becker, Allen III, & Guzman 2008). While nonresearch partnerships may not be fraught with the same risk of human rights violations, there are parallels to the challenges presented in such partnerships. Thus, the principles from CBPR, identified by Israel and colleagues in 2008, prove useful for helping frame interactions and expectations of colleges and nonprofit organizations (NPOs) when working on community engagement projects.

The following principles and purpose of CBPR, as applied to community engagement projects between colleges and nonprofit organizations, will be discussed:

1. CBPR recognizes community as a unit of identity.

Israel et al. (2008) argued that communities are distinguished by common symbols, values and norms, interests, and needs, as well as the emotional connectivity of community members. Such communities may be defined by geographical boundaries (e.g., Appalachia) or a shared identity (e.g., religious affiliation or sexual orientation). While communities often have a wide variety of resources available within their membership, CBPR facilitates the partnering of those sources with agencies outside of the geographical or ideological boundaries of a given community. Using a CBPR approach in a college-community partnership can help participants from both sides of the partnership recognize and value the resources the other has.

By mutually engaging in the development of a project, CBPR allows those with whom the project will be implemented to decide which characteristics of their group identity are relevant. As an example, in an effort to improve the diets of rural Appalachians, Tessaro and her colleagues (2006) developed a computer-based intervention that mimicked a cooking show, recognizing that low literacy, which is a cultural characteristic of Appalachia, might have otherwise prevented some of the target audience from being able to engage in and benefit from the intervention. Through focus groups with the target population, the authors learned that weight loss was a stronger reason for the participants to change their dietary behaviors than was avoiding heart disease, although the participants also recognized the increasing threat of heart disease due to changes in society. Learning about the importance of various factors allowed the academic partners to develop an individually tailored project that meets the different needs of the participants.

2. CBPR builds on the strengths and resources within the community.

Existing resources within a community include the skills and assets of the individuals who comprise the community as well as the networks within the community, and the mediating structures such as churches and other organizations where members of the community can come together. The goal of CBPR is to support and expand the existing resources within a community to enable its members to work better together to accomplish their collective goals. NPOs bring a wealth of resources, skills, connections, and people to any college-community partnership, and those resources need to be identified and built upon in community engagement projects. Similarly, faculty have access to a host of resources, including scholarly expertise, grant finding and grant proposal writing ability, college financial support, and, oftentimes, encouragement or a mandate to engage in community-based projects.

Contrary to the common practice of abandoning projects once data gathering is complete in non-CBPR work, the goal of CBPR studies is to have community members or organizations take over the project. After the implementation of a CBPR project to reduce adolescent substance abuse, community members in Lawrence, Kansas continued to seek funding and develop initiatives to accomplish the coalition's goals (Fawcett et al. 1995). The CBPR project had helped build community members' resources, and the community members were able to continue to instigate, fund, and implement initiatives after the faculty partner's funding was gone. When faculty share resources (e.g., grant searching mechanisms) with non-profit partners (as outlined in chapter 3), the community organization may be empowered to sustain projects beyond the partnership.

3. CBPR facilitates collaborative, equitable partnership in all research phases and involves an empowering and power-sharing process that attends to social inequalities.

All members of a CBPR study work together to define the problem, collect and interpret the data, and decide on the appropriate course of action given the findings. Because community members have not had the same opportunities and experience as the researchers or experts, it is vital that researchers identify that inequality in such a way as to encourage community members to provide information as to their key concerns. Similarly, faculty and nonprofit partners should work together to identify the goals of a project, and neither side's agenda should take precedence over the other's. To that end, faculty need to be up front with nonprofit partners regarding what they need to get out of the partnership (i.e., products that count toward tenure and promotion), and nonprofit leaders need to be aware that, while the faculty may be able to offer pure service to the NPO, better outcomes will be generated when both sides are aware of the other's needs and are cognizant of helping all partners achieve collective and individually useful ends.

4. CBPR promotes colearning and capacity building among all partners.

Colearning involves reciprocal sharing of information, skills, and capacity between faculty and nonprofit partners. Of particular importance are the locally held beliefs and norms within the community that may influence various aspects of the CBPR process, including recruitment and retention of partners (and participants in research-focused projects) and willingness to engage in projects or interventions. By sharing knowledge with all partners, CBPR is more likely to be applicable to other goals and processes that partners are involved in. College-community partnerships may focus on one aspect of the missions and goals of the various partners, and by sharing information and facilitating colearning (i.e., learning that is not flowing solely from the faculty to the NPO or vice versa), all partners will be more aware of the challenges to accomplishing that goal as well as identifying potential avenues for future collaboration.

5. CBPR integrates and achieves a balance between research and action for the mutual benefit of all partners.

It is not enough to gather a deep body of knowledge regarding the state of community in a CBPR study. It is vital that the knowledge inform action aimed at improving the lot of community partners. In a reinforcing spiral, knowledge informs actions, which in turn provides more knowledge regarding the issue of concern in the community. While CBPR may not involve action being taken (depending on the will of the community partners), with this approach comes the implicit assumption of willingness and commitment to translate research into action for the benefit of all partners involved.

Findings from non-CBPR studies are typically disseminated via academic, peer-reviewed journal articles to stimulate the interest of a group with adequate resources to translate the researchers' findings into action. On the other hand, CBPR projects recognize that, while publishing results is a good thing, it is not the ultimate goal of such work. Members of the Seattle Partners for Healthy Communities stated that getting something published was a major accomplishment when asked about it, but they rarely listed publishing when the interviewers asked them about the successes of the project (Eisinger and Senturia 2001). Similarly (and related to point 3), while publishable outputs may not be a main focus for nonprofit partners, bearing in mind that such products are crucial for faculty success, college-community partnerships will be more successful if both sides are aware of the need and value of publication arising from the collaboration. Not only does publication contribute to faculty success, but it also can enhance a nonprofit organization's visibility to stakeholders and potential funders.

6. CBPR involves systems development through a cyclical and iterative process.

By developing the systems necessary to implement successful CBPR, the necessary competencies are set in place to facilitate an iterative cycle wherein research informs action, which increases knowledge, and so on. A key example of this iterative process was discussed by Minkler and Pies (2004) when community members were hired to do community organizing work around the issue of family planning. A health educator on the team realized that the eight women hired to do the work took their positions for the money, not because they felt strongly about promoting family planning practices. Upon that realization, the health educator dropped the formal agenda of the agency and worked with the women to identify the major needs of the residents of the neighborhood. The group then worked to address sanitation issues and the presence of drug dealers in the area. When they realized that the agency truly cared about the needs of the community, the women sought to learn about the family planning that had been the initial agenda; many came to see the benefits for their community and helped the agency meet its original goals. By starting where the community was, the faculty partner was able to help members meet their needs and ultimately the purposes for which the project had been started as well.

In college-community partnerships, when working together on an agreed-upon project, both sides of the partnership should seek to understand the most important objectives for the other partners. While the needs of one partner may not be the initial focus, successful and sustainable college-community partnership projects will, ultimately, work toward ends that address the missions of all parties involved and produce outcomes that count for all involved. Through an iterative process of working to meet the NPO's needs and then using information from that process to create teaching and/or learning opportunities for students, grant writing opportunities for faculty (and their NPO partners), and/or peer-reviewed publications regarding the project, both faculty and nonprofit partners can receive needed benefits from the project.

7. CBPR disseminates findings and knowledge gained to all partners and involves all partners in the dissemination process.

As part of the dissemination process in CBPR projects, all partners are recognized as coauthors in the creation of the knowledge.

Furthermore, the knowledge gained should be used to inform action. While employees and volunteers in NPOs may not have extensive scientific writing experience and may see little personal or professional benefit from producing peer-reviewed publications, they should plan to work with their faculty partners to develop means of disseminating the results of the project. Both sides of the partnership should work to ensure that the presentation and publication of project results inform future actions and projects implemented by the partners. Careful attention to future opportunities can guide the dissemination of project results and save time and energy in future collaborative efforts by the college-community partners.

8. CBPR requires a long-term process and commitment to sustainability.

The commitment to work together with community partners must extend beyond the data-collection phase or the funding cycle when conducting CBPR. The relationships developed through CBPR are at least partly based on the agreed-upon outcomes (i.e., actions) to be expected through the project. The researchers cannot abandon the community because they are done with what they intended to do there. It is crucial to CBPR that the researchers do what they can to accomplish the goals they agreed to with the community member when they first came in. Similarly, when faculty partner with NPOs, they may have a limited time frame for implementing a project (e.g., one semester if it is a course-based service-learning project with student involvement) or limited funding (e.g., a grant to fund the project).

By basing college-community partnerships on the CBPR model, faculty should plan either to work with the nonprofit partner beyond the scope of a given project or should create a careful exit strategy so as not to leave the organization in the lurch. The careful exit strategy should be preplanned by being written into the MOU in the Dissolution Plan section.

Conversely, nonprofit leaders need to be aware that faculty have limited time and energy to give to efforts that do not contribute significantly to their teaching or research objectives. Thus, sustainable college-community projects need to consider means of continuing beyond the assistance of the faculty partner (e.g., through efforts to secure funding from foundations that support the mission of the NPO rather than requiring perpetual donation of time from the faculty partner to keep the project going), while at the same time developing outcomes that meet both partners' needs. When partners from both sides receive personal and professional benefit from the partnership and pay careful attention to setting up future collaborations, college-community partnerships will be more satisfying and productive for all involved.

While not all college-community partnerships involve research, they inherently involve participation from community members. Principles from community-based participatory research can be easily applied to any college-community partnership. By actively involving stakeholders from both the college and the nonprofit organization in the development, implementation, and dissemination of a project, the objectives of all involved are more likely to be met, and projects emerging from such partnerships will be more sustainable and beneficial to the constituents served by both the nonprofit organization and the college.

Sustainability of Community Engagement Projects, Programs, and Services

As discussed above, sustainability of community engagement projects, programs, and services initiated through college-community partnerships should be paramount for a variety of reasons, starting with ethics and ending with the achievement of the nonprofit partner's mission. Ensuring sustainability starts with a clear and complete memorandum of understanding and ends with effective communication between all partners.

Ethical Standards for Nonprofit Leaders and Faculty Partners

Besides ethics related to human subjects research and community-based participatory research, the nonprofit management profession has established key ethical standards for different areas of nonprofit management and leadership, including program evaluation, fundraising, and volunteer management. All faculty partners and nonprofit leaders, professional or volunteer, as well as students, should be thoroughly acquainted with and practice these ethical standards, a list and description of which follows.

American Evaluation Association (AEA): Guiding Principles for Evaluators

When collaborating on a community engagement project related to program evaluation, faculty partners and nonprofit leaders need to adhere to, as well as educate students on, the guiding principles for evaluators. Key guiding principles that apply to college-community evaluative projects include the following: conducting systematic, data-based inquiry; ensuring competence; demonstrating honesty and integrity, especially in interpreting data and reporting findings; demonstrating respect for people; and taking into account the diversity of general and public interest (American Evaluation Association [AEA] 2014). For a full review of the American Evaluation Association (AEA): Guiding Principles for Evaluators, visit

http://www.eval.org/p/cm/ld/fid=51

Association of Fundraising Professionals (AFP): Code of Ethical Principles and Standards

Faculty partners and nonprofit leaders, when collaborating on a community engagement project related to fundraising, need to realize that, ultimately, fundraising success is based on the ability to build positive relationships over time, which in turn is entirely based on ethical interactions between two or more people. AFP encourages fundraisers to practice with "integrity, honesty, truthfulness, and adherence to the absolute obligation to safeguard the public trust" (Association of Fundraising Professionals [AFP] 2014a). Public trust is maintained by honoring donor intent, being transparent, maintaining confidentiality, and not working on commission (AFP 2014a). For a full review of the Association of Fundraising Professionals (AFP): Code of Ethical Principles and Standards, visit

http://www.afpnet.org/Ethics/EnforcementDetail.cfm? ItemNumber=3261

Association of Fundraising Professionals (AFP): Donor Bill of Rights

AFP has also created a Donor Bill of Rights that further encourages those fundraising on behalf of a nonprofit organization to ensure that prospects and donors are informed of the organization's mission and the identity of those serving on the organization's governing board, have access to the organization's recent financial records, have assurance that their gifts will be used as intended and that confidentiality will be maintained (AFP, 2014b). Donors also have the right to know "whether those seeking donations are volunteers (e.g., students, faculty partners), employees of the organization, or hired solicitors" (AFP 2014b). For a full review of the Association of Fundraising Professionals (AFP): Donor Bill of Rights, visit

http://www.afpnet.org/ethics/enforcementDetail.cfm?
ItemNumber=3359

Council for Certification in Volunteer Administration (CCVA): Professional Ethics in Volunteer Administration

Faculty partners and nonprofit leaders need to realize that any college-community partnership that engages students in a community engagement project that benefits the nonprofit organization with no financial benefit to the students makes them volunteers. In essence, the faculty member becomes the codirector of volunteer management for the nonprofit organization in partnership with the nonprofit leader. When working with students on community engagement projects the following core ethical values in volunteer administration should be adhered to: citizenship and philanthropy; respect; responsibility; caring; justice and fairness; and trustworthiness (CCVA 2014). For a full review of the Council for Certification in Volunteer Administration Professional Ethics in Volunteer Administration visit

http://www.cvacert.org/professional.htm

Engaged scholars should strongly consider becoming aware of the professional and scholarly work in volunteer administration, such as the Council for Certification in Volunteer Administration, the Certified Volunteer Administrator (CVA) credential, the Central Indiana Association of Volunteer Administrators (CIAVA), and other volunteer management professional associations, as well as the International Journal of Volunteer Administration. Developing high-quality college-community partnerships where students significantly achieve learning outcomes as assessed through formative and summative academic assessment that are also highly satisfying experiences is as much the faculty partners' volunteer administration skills as it is pedagogy (i.e., techniques to teach youth) or andragogy (i.e., techniques to teach adults).

References

American Evaluation Association [AEA]. *Guiding principles for evaluators.* (2014) Retrieved from http://www.eval.org/p/cm/ld/fid=51

Association of Fundraising Professionals [AFP]. *Code of ethical principles and standards.* (2014a) Retrieved from http://www.afpnet. org/Ethics/EnforcementDetail.cfm?ItemNumber=3261

Association of Fundraising Professionals [AFP]. *Donor bill of rights.* (2014b) Retrieved from http://www.afpnet.org/ethics/enforcement Detail.cfm?ItemNumber=3359

Council for Certification in Volunteer Administration [CCVA]. *Professional ethics in volunteer administration.* (2014) Retrieved from http://www.cvacert.org/professional.htm

Eisinger, A., and K. D. Senturia. "Doing Community-Driven Research: An Evaluative Description of Seattle Partners for Healthy Communities." *Journal of Urban Health* 78 (2001): 519–534.

Fawcett, S. B.; A. Paine-Andrews; V. T. Francisco; J. A. Schultz; K. P. Richter; R. K. Lewis; E. L. Williams; K. J. Harris; J. Y. Berkley; J. L. Fisher; C. M. Lopez. "Using empowerment theory in collaborative partnerships for community health and development." *American Journal of Community Psychology* 23(5) (1995), 677–697.

Israel, B.A.; A. J. Schulz; E. A. Parker; A. B. Becker; A. J. Allen; J. R. Guzman. "Critical Issues in developing and following CBPR principles." In *Community-based participatory research for health: From process to outcomes.* ed. M. Minkler (San Francisco: Jossey-Bass, 2008), 47–66.

Minkler, M., and C. Pies. (2004). "Ethical issues and practical dilemmas in community organization and community participation." In *Community organizing and community building for health,* second ed. M. Minkler (New Brunswick: Rutgers University Press, 2004), 116–133.

Tessaro, I.; S. Rye; L. Parker.; K. Trangsrud; C. Mangone; S. McCrone; N. Leslie. "Cookin' Up Health: Developing a Nutrition Intervention for a Rural Appalachian Population." *Health Promotion Practice* 7 (2006): 252–257.

US Department of Health and Human Services. *Title 45 Public Welfare: Part 46 Protection of Human Subjects.* (45 CFR 46, 2014) Retrieved from http://www.hhs.gov/ohrp/humansubjects/ guidance/45cfr46.html#46.102

Resources

American Evaluation Association: Guiding Principles for Evaluators
http://www.eval.org/p/cm/ld/fid=51

Association of Fundraising Professionals: Code of Ethical Principles and Standards
http://www.afpnet.org/Ethics/EnforcementDetail.cfm? ItemNumber=3261

Association of Fundraising Professionals: Donor Bill of Rights
http://www.afpnet.org/ethics/enforcementDetail.cfm? ItemNumber=3359

Council for Certification in Volunteer Administration: Professional Ethics in Volunteer Administration
http://www.cvacert.org/professional.htm

DePauw University Institutional Review Board
http://www.depauw.edu/offices/academic-affairs/ human-participants-and-animal-use/guidelines-for-using- human-sub/

US Department of Health and Human Services. *Title 45 Public Welfare: Part 46 Protection of Human Subjects.* (45 CFR 46, 2014) http://www.hhs.gov/ohrp/humansubjects/guidance/45cfr46.html#46.102

APPENDIX A
Glossary of Terms

The included glossary of terms comes from the work of our colleagues, the 2010–2011 Indiana Campus Compact Faculty Fellows, as found in the following publication:

Eisenhauer, M.J.; N. B. Marthakis; J. Jamison; M. Mattson. eds. *Charting the Course for Service-Learning: From Curriculum Considerations to Advocacy, A Faculty Development Workbook.* (Indianapolis: Indiana Campus Compact, 2011).

AmeriCorps— AmeriCorps is a U.S. federal government program under the Corporation for National and Community Service that was created under President Bill Clinton by the National and Community Service Trust Act of 1993. Often referred to as the domestic Peace Corps, AmeriCorps places AmeriCorps Members across the U.S. to assist with focus areas such as public education to environmental clean-up.

Campus funding—funding opportunities, often in the form of grants that are offered through campus departments or units, such as seed grant opportunities through the Provost.

Civic engagement—acting upon a heightened sense of responsibility to one's community through one or more of the following: learning from others, self, and environment to develop informed perspectives on social issues; recognizing and appreciating human diversity and commonality; behaving, and working through controversy, with civility; participating actively in public life, public problem solving, and community service; assuming leadership and membership roles in organizations; developing empathy, ethics, values, and sense of social responsibility; promoting social justice locally and globally (adapted from www.terpimpact.umd.edu).

Co-construction of curriculum—collaboration between and among faculty, community partners and students to develop and plan the course so that the needs of everyone involved are met through the learning outcomes, the experiential component and the assessment.

Community asset mapping—a needs-assessment technique that involves the process of intentionally identifying the human, material, financial, entrepreneurial and other resources in a community.

Community forum—a needs-assessment technique that involves inviting interested community members to a large group meeting to voice their concerns and ideas about community needs and implementing a project to address an identified need or needs.

Community partner—the agency, organization or entity with whom the student and faculty collaborate. The main liaison may be an individual or a group of individuals.

Confidentiality—an ethical responsibility to keep secure information and identities.

Continuing Education Unit (CEU)—one CEU is the number of contact hours of participation in organized continuing education/ training experience under responsible, qualified direction and instruction.

Disclosure—*a*n ethical responsibility to share information that has the potential to influence or impact the workplace or experience.

Dispositions—*a* set of attitudes, moods and beliefs.

Dynamic assessment—*i*nteractive assessment tools often incorporating open-ended questions.

Engaged Scholar—a faculty member who redefines faculty scholarly work from application of academic expertise to community engaged scholarship that involves the faculty member in a reciprocal partnership with the community that is interdisciplinary and integrates faculty roles of teaching, research, and service. Additionally, an engaged scholar participates in the collaboration between academics and individuals outside the academy - knowledge professionals and the lay public (local, regional/state, national, global) - for the mutually beneficial exchange of knowledge and resources in a context of partnership and reciprocity (New England Resource Center for Higher Education).

Entrance/Exit Interview—an informal or formal conversation between parties to assess the needs, skills and expectations for the service-learning project.

External grants—funding opportunities offered from external organizations and agencies.

Face-to-Face Asks—fundraising that is done in person.

Faculty Fellows Program—a year-long fellowship program that brings together service-learning faculty for partnership, learning, and reflection on engaged scholarship.

Federal Work-Study—Federally funded program that allows colleges and universities to create campus based employment programs for financial aid recipients. Colleges and universities are required to spend 7 percent of federal work study funds on community service positions.

Focus group—a needs assessment technique that involves inviting interested community members to a small-group meeting to voice their concerns and ideas about community needs and implementing a project to address an identified need or needs.

Foundation Office—the office on a campus that often oversees fundraising initiatives from a campus-wide perspective.

Grants Officer—staff member within the Sponsored Research and/or Contracts/Grants office on a campus who is responsible for assisting faculty/staff with funding opportunities and proposal development.

HIPPA—Health Insurance Portability and Accountability Act

Institutional Review Board (IRB)—the formal committee established by an institution to review all protocols and procedures used in research and to uphold ethical, moral and academic principles.

Key informant interview— a needs-assessment technique that involves an interview with an individual identified as key within the community or community organization to gain insight into the community and the community's needs.

Liability waiver—a release or giving up of a right or rights, such as releasing an organization from responsibility for harm or damage that may occur from participating in an activity.

Memorandum of Understanding (MOU)—an agreement between parties that outlines the roles, responsibilities, services to be provided and expected outcomes.

National Society for Experiential Education—National Society for Experiential Education (NSEE) is a nonprofit membership association of educators, businesses, and community leaders. Founded in 1971, NSEE also serves as a national resource center for the development and improvement of experiential education programs nationwide.

Needs assessment—systematic process to determine and document a community's or a community organization's needs.

Op.Ed.—is an abbreviation of "opposite the editorial page." It is a newspaper article that expresses the opinion of a named writer that is often unaffiliated with the newspaper.

Preflection—"a strategy designed as a tool to enhance and enrich the reflection process. It is actually a reflective session that is held prior to the service experience. Students are encouraged to imagine what the experience will be like and to express any feelings they might have as they anticipate their involvement. Comments are recorded and are reviewed with the students after the service has been completed. Being able to look back on their pre-service thoughts and feelings and compare and contrast them to the reality of the actual experience has the effect of promoting and focusing discussion, and deepening insights into the relevance of the service for all participants." From: Falk, D. (1995). Preflection: A strategy for enhancing reflection. *NSEE Quarterly*, 13.

Press Release—a formally prepared announcement or news item circulated to the media.

Reciprocity of relationship—the explicit understanding of mutual benefit between and among all parties.

Reserve funds—a pool of excess funds that often have been developed by indirect cost recovery from multiple grants.

Segal Education Award— Congress established the National Service Trust to provide an AmeriCorps Education Award for AmeriCorps members who successfully complete service in AmeriCorps. AmeriCorps Education Awards can be used to pay educational expenses at qualified institutions of higher education, for educational training, or to repay qualified student loans. The AmeriCorps Education Award must be used seven years after the term of service has ended.

Service Engagement – is any endeavor that brings the community into the campus and the campus into the community, reciprocally, often addressing a social concern. Forms of service engagement include:

- service-learning, co-curricular community service, and volunteerism; and

- some internships and field experiences.

The sum of these activities leads to a campus that is fully engaged with the community. Service engagement is also referred to as "civic engagement" by many national organizations (Jamison and McCracken 2007).

Service-Learning—is a credit-bearing, educational experience in which students participate in an organized service activity that meets identified community needs and reflect on the service activity in such a way as to gain further understanding of course content, a broader appreciation of the discipline, and an enhanced sense of civic responsibility (Bringle and Hatcher 1996).

Social indicators—a needs-assessment technique that uses statistics from already published reports to determine a community's or community organization's needs.

Strategic Plan—a statement that defines an organization's desired future, how it is going to get there, and how it will know if it got there.

Survey— a needs-assessment technique that involves asking a sample of community members standardized questions about their knowledge, attitudes, and behaviors regarding a need and their reactions to implementing a project to address the need.

SWOT analysis— a needs-assessment technique that audits the situational factors and forces in the internal and external environments that likely will impact aspects of a service-learning project.

Transactional partnerships— "are limited in scope, short-term in commitment, and ask little of partners in terms of long-term change." (Jones and Palmerton 2010, 166).

Transformational partnerships— "require that, as a result of the relationship, both partners change through an ongoing commitment to a goal larger than each." (Jones and Palmerton 2010,166).

CPSIA information can be obtained at www.ICGtesting.com
Printed in the USA
BVOW01s1328080315

390783BV00018B/623/P